Fell

Official
Know-It-All
Guide™

Contract

Bridge

Your Absolute,
Quintessential,
All You Wanted to Know,
Complete Guide

Alan Truscott

Frederick Fell Publishers, Inc.

Fell's Official Know-It-All Guide
Frederick Fell Publishers, Inc.
2131 Hollywood Boulevard, Suite 305
Hollywood, Florida 33020
954-925-5242
e-mail: fellpub@aol.com
Visit our Web site at www.fellpub.com

Copyright © 2001, 1993, 1982, 1959 by Alan Truscott
All rights reserved.

Library of Congress Cataloging-in-Publication Data
Truscott, Alan F.
  Fell's official know-it-all guide to bridge / by Alan Truscott.
    p. cm.
Rev. ed. of: Contract bridge. c1993
  ISBN 0-88391-063-2 (alk. paper)
1. Contract bridge. I. Truscott, Alan F. Contract bridge. II. Title.
  GV1282.3 .T745 2001
  795.41'5--dc21

                                                      2001001269

    2 3 4 5 6 7 8 9 0

Cover Design Elena Solis
Interior Design Lora Horton

Contract Bridge

Of all card games, Bridge, or to give it its full name, Contract Bridge, is undoubtedly the one most played the worldover. It is equally true that once a bridge player, always a bridge player, and no other card game will do.

This book is an introduction to all phases of the game, and is suitable for beginners and intermediate players. The author, Alan Truscott, is one of the world's greatest bridge writers. He has been Bridge Editor of the *New York Times* since 1964, is the author of many books, and is a former British international player. This edition of a book first published in England has been completely updated by him.

Table of Contents

Introduction

Every year more and more people around the world play Contract Bridge. You can play it at any age, and in the face of many physical handicaps. Besides being a challenge to the intellect it is a challenge to the competitive instinct - the urge to win. Above all it is a social game —- it is fun.

There are now, probably, a quarter of a million players in China, and Eastern Europe is catching up. In any major city in the world a bridge player can find a club where he will be welcomed.

The ancestor game of Whist began in the sixteenth century, and took a giant step forward about 1740. A London lawyer named Edmund Hoyle wrote the first book on the game, and his rules for this and other games became so well known that we still say "According to Hoyle".

A century ago Whist was undergoing an evolution that ended in 1925 when Contract Bridge was codified by a man famous in another area: Harold Vanderbilt, twice winner of the America's Cup and the codifier of the Rules of the Road for sailing vessels.

Vanderbilt's game was "Rubber Bridge", which is now relatively rare in North America. As a rubber may take a long time, most players prefer "Four-deal Bridge", which is also called Chicago. The change is equivalent to the introduction of the tiebreaker in tennis, and is explained on page 15.

Another important form of the game is "duplicate", which means that all deals are played at least twice and the results compared. This is the way that all competitive bridge is played, from the local level up to world championships.

This book is in three parts. Chapters 1 and 2 deal with the mechanics of the game - the rules and the scoring. Chapters 3-9 inclusive deal with the bidding; and Chapters 10, 11 and 12 deal with the play of the cards.

If you have never played bridge, you are advised to read the book fairly quickly, and try to grasp the general principles. Do not try to memorize in detail all the longer sequences of bidding given: they are included partly as examples, and partly for reference. Later you can reread any topics you feel you have not completely understood.

Readers who have already played some bridge should start at Chapter 3. Do not on any account miss this chapter, which gives the amended point-count on which the bidding in the later chapters is based.

♣ ♦ ♥ ♠

Chapter 1

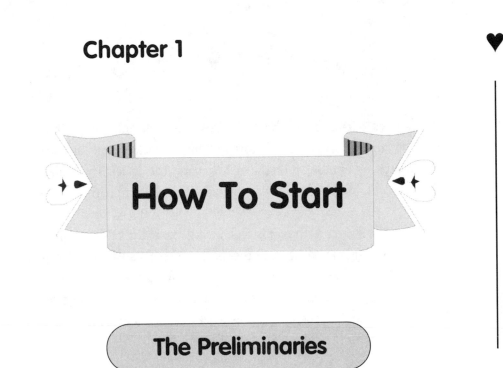

How To Start

The Preliminaries

You are going to play your first rubber – the first, we hope, of many. You need three other players, four chairs and a table. On the table you put two decks of cards (preferably with different colored backs) and four bridge score-pads and four pencils. At a pinch one deck of cards, one pencil and an odd piece of paper will do.

Spread one deck face downward across the table so that each player can draw a card. The players who draw the two highest cards play together as partners against the other two. the player with the highest card will be the dealer, and can choose which seat he wishes to sit in, and which deck of cards he wishes to deal with. His partner sits opposite him, and the opponents occupy the other seats. (If two players cut cards of the same value, the *rank* of the suits decides – *see under Auction, page 3.*

Shuffle and Deal

The dealer's left-hand opponent shuffles the deck and passes it to his partner, who cuts the cards. He does this by lifting a block of cards off the deck, face downwards, and putting it on the table towards the dealer. The dealer then completes the cut, bringing the cards originally at the bottom of the deck to the top.

The dealer now deals all the cards, first giving one to his left-hand opponent and then continuing clockwise until the cards are exhausted and each player has thirteen. Meanwhile the dealer's partner is shuffling the spare deck, which he puts on his right. (The old saw runs: "If you're not demented quite, place the cards upon your right.") The deal passes clockwise in rotation, and the spare deck is now ready for the cut and deal on the next hand.

The Auction

An auction at bridge is exactly like any other auction: all concerned are entitled to bid, and the auction continues until nobody wishes to bid any higher. The final bid is the winner.

A bid at bridge is an offer to take a certain number of tricks with the help of your partner's hand. The number of tricks bid is always the number of tricks *more than six* to be made, so that a bid of "one" is an offer to take seven tricks. A bid of "seven" is an offer to take all the thirteen possible tricks after partner's hand (for an explanation of "trick", see below, in section on the play).

The player who wins the auction has the right to choose which suit shall be the trump suit, or master suit. During the play a player who has no card in the suit led may if he wishes play a trump; this will win the trick unless another player plays a higher trump. The right to choose the trump suit is a great advantage. Sometimes a player may prefer "no-trump," however, when each trick is won by the highest card played in the suit led.

When you make a bid, you name your proposed trump suit as well as the number of tricks you are offering to try to make. So a bid of "four hearts" means: "I will try to take ten tricks with hearts as trump with the help of my partner's hand."

For the purposes of the auction, the suits rank in alphabetical order from the bottom up, with notrump as the highest:

* Notrump
* Spades
* Hearts
* Diamonds
* Clubs

3

Thus if the last bid made was one heart, you could bid one spade or one no-trump, which rank higher than hearts. But if you want to bid clubs or diamonds you would have to bid two clubs or two diamonds at least. Note that it is not necessary to make only minimum bids. It will often be a good idea to jump the auction to a high level quickly.

A Sample Hand

To help understand the way the bidding and play proceed, let us suppose we have dealt the following hand. Do not at this stage worry about the reason for any bid or play.

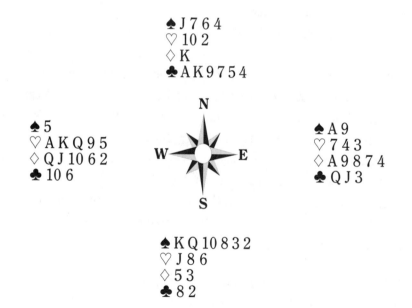

4

North and South are partners against East and West. West was the dealer and has the first bid. He bids "one heart." It is now North's turn, and he wishes to bid clubs. As clubs rank lower than hearts, he bids "two clubs." East wishes to bid his diamonds, and as diamonds rank higher than clubs, he is able to bid "two diamonds." South bids "two spades" (higher than diamonds) and West supports his partner by bidding three diamonds. North could bid simply "three spades," which, as we shall see later, is a "game" bid. East perseveres with "five diamonds," which is also a "game" bid. South says, "pass," and so does West; but North does not give up easily, so he bids "five spades."

If, when it is your turn, the opponents have bid to a contract that you think will fail, you can "double." This greatly increases the reward for success and the penalty for failure. East now announces "double," because he thinks his side can defeat the opposing contract of five spades. South, West and North all say "pass," and the auction is over.

If either North or South still felt convinced that their contract of five spades would succeed, he could "redouble." This would roughly double, once again, the number of points to be won and lost on the hand.

Note that once any bid has been made, three consecutive "passes" end the auction. If, however, the first four calls in the auction are "pass," the hand is "thrown in" or "passed out." A new hand is dealt by the next player in rotation (in four-deal bridge, the same player redeals).

The bidding on the above hand can be tabulated for convenience in the following way:

West	North	East	South
1 ♡	2 ♣	2 ◇	2 ♠
3 ◇	4 ♠	5 ◇	pass
pass	5 ♠	double	pass
pass	pass		

The final bid is five spades, which has been doubled. So five spades doubled is the *contract*. North and South have, therefore, to try to make eleven tricks with spades as the trump suit. North and South are the *declaring* side, and East and West are the *defenders*. South is called the declarer, because he first bid the spade suit, and it will be his duty and privilege to play the North and South hands in combination. North will be the "dummy," and takes no part in the play of the hand. Usually the player who makes the final bid is the declarer, but this is not so if, as in our example, this player is merely supporting his partner's choice of suit.

♣ The Play

The player on declarer's left starts the proceedings by putting a card face upwards on the table. This is the "opening lead," and in our example West makes the opening lead of the king of hearts.

After the opening lead has been made, the dummy puts his cards face upwards on the table so that all can see. He should put the trumps, if any, on his right.

Now South has to play, in the correct turn, both from dummy and his own hand. He therefore plays the two of hearts from dummy, East plays the three of hearts and South the six of hearts. West's king of hearts has won the trick, so he collects the four cards played and puts them in a neat pile face downwards in front of him. As West won the trick, it is his duty to lead to the next trick. He now leads the ace of hearts, which also wins the trick, as each of the other three hands is compelled to follow suit with a small heart.

It is still West's lead, and he can see that if he plays a third heart the dummy hand, which now has no more hearts, will play a spade, which, being a trump, will win the trick. West therefore leads the queen of diamonds. South has no choice but to play dummy's king of diamonds, and East puts on the ace of diamonds. The ace of diamonds wins the trick when South follows with the three of diamonds.

As East won the last trick, he now leads the queen of clubs. South and West play small cards, and South then puts on the king of clubs from dummy, which takes the trick. As dummy won the trick, South must play from the dummy; he decides to lead the four of spades. East plays the nine of spades, South the king of spades and West the five of spades.

At this point South has made two tricks and the defenders have made three tricks. The remaining cards are as shown in the following diagram:

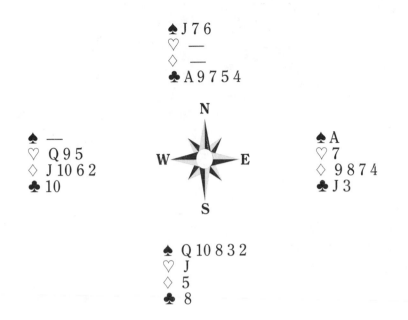

♠ J 7 6
♡ —
◇ —
♣ A 9 7 5 4

♠ —
♡ Q 9 5
◇ J 10 6 2
♣ 10

N
W　E
S

♠ A
♡ 7
◇ 9 8 7 4
♣ J 3

♠ Q 10 8 3 2
♡ J
◇ 5
♣ 8

South sees that he can trump his losing heart in dummy, and also his losing diamond. Dummy's ace of clubs will win a trick, after which he can trump clubs himself. The only trick he can possibly lose is to the ace of spades, so he exposes his remaining cards and claims seven out of the last eight tricks. The defenders look at declarers' cards, and agree that South's claim is a just one.

South has made only nine tricks when he had contracted for eleven, and the penalty is increased because the contract was doubled. As we shall see when we do the scoring, East and West gain 300 points.

Following the play of a bridge hand from a diagram is not easy for the inexperienced player. The best plan is to make an oblique pencil stroke through each card on the diagram as it is played. It is then easy to see at each stage which cards still remain in the four hands, and the pencil marks can be erased afterwards.

Chapter 2

Objects And Scoring

The Contract Principle

The auction is not merely an attempt to outbid the opponents. Each partnership, even if their opponents are silent, will try to bid up to a high contract if the value of their own hands permits. The reason for this is most important:

You only count towards game tricks that you have bid and made.

For example, if the bid is two hearts and ten tricks are made, the two extra tricks, or overtricks, are of little value. It would have been far more valuable for the declaring side if the bid had been four hearts.

It is vital from the start to remember which bids will win your side a game in one hand. They are:

* **Three Notrump**
* **Four Spades**
* **Four Hearts**
* **Five Diamonds**
* **Five Clubs**

Whenever possible you and your partner should try to bid up to one of these contracts. A smaller contract will earn a "part-score," and sometimes a game can be achieved by making two or three part-scores.

Sometimes it pays to go beyond a game contract. If your side is very powerful, you may be able to bid "six," contracting for twelve tricks. If you succeed, you score a small slam, sometimes called a little slam, which is both exciting and profitable. This is quite common, but it is only very rarely that you should attempt a grand slam, for which you must contract for all thirteen tricks by bidding "seven."

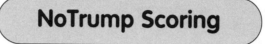

NoTrump Scoring

Each trick in a notrump contract scores 30, except the first trick which counts 40. Thus three notrump provides the necessary 100 points to make a game (40 + 30 + 30), and this is the commonest contract of all.

10

As three notrump is sufficient for a game, bids of four notrump and higher are rare. It might be necessary to make such a bid to outbid the opponents, but it is more likely to happen if the players are trying for a slam. Bidding and making six notrump earns a large bonus for a small slam; and bidding and making a grand slam of seven notrump gets an even larger bonus.

Major-Suit Scoring

Spades and hearts are the major suits, and each trick bid and made in a major suit counts 30 points towards game. A bid of four is therefore necessary to gain the 100 points needed for a game. Four spades and four hearts are common contracts, but it is unusual to play in five spades or five hearts: these are more than required for a game, but not enough to earn a slam bonus.

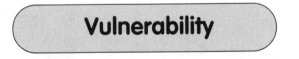

Minor-Suit Scoring

Each trick bid and made in clubs and diamonds, the minor suits, counts 20 points. A bid of five is thus enough for game, but this seldom occurs. Rather than bid for eleven tricks with a minor suit as trump, it is usually better to try for a game in no-trump, which requires only nine tricks.

Vulnerability

When you are "vulnerable" the tension increases. The reward for making a game or slam is bigger, but the penalty for failure increases. When you are vulnerable you must therefore be more cautious in making a bid that you think may result in failure if the bidding ends.

11

In four-deal bridge, nobody is vulnerable at the start. The dealer and his partner are vulnerable on the second and third deals, and everybody is vulnerable on the fourth deal. Bonuses are scored like this: 500 for making a vulnerable game; and 300 for making a non-vulnerable game. Making a part-score (something less than game) on the fourth deal earns 100.

Each deal is scored separately, but a part-score carries over to subsequent deals, unless eliminated by an opposing game, and may be combined with one (or more) later part-scores to make a game.

♣

Penalties

When a contract fails, the defenders collect the penalty shown in the following table. There is no need to learn it: after playing for a time you will find you have absorbed it without effort.

The progression in the table of penalties is easy to follow. Undoubled penalties increase by 50 and 100 according to vulnerability. Doubled penalties, after the first trick, increase by 200 and 300 a trick according to vulnerability. Redoubled penalties are exactly twice the corresponding doubled penalty; they will be very rare indeed unless you play in reckless company.

	NOT VULNERABLE		VULNERABLE	
Contract goes:	*Undoubled*	*Doubled*	*Undoubled*	*Doubled*
1 down	50	100	100	200
2 down	100	300	200	500
3 down	150	500	300	800
4 down	200	800	400	1,100
5 down	250	1,100	500	1,400
6 down	300	1,400	600	1,700

12

Success When Doubled

If you make your contract when you have been doubled you get a bonus of 50 and the points you would normally have scored are doubled. This can be vitally important. A contract of two hearts, bid and made, scores 60 points; it is a part-score, and takes you part of the way towards game. But two hearts *doubled*, bid and made, scores 60 + 60 and is worth a game in itself. If this happens to you, you have been "doubled into game": the opponents will be livid, and may even be rude to each other.

Remember that the extra 50 points "for the insult" do not count towards game, so that two clubs doubled and made, for example, counts only 80 points towards the 100 required for game.

♦

A redoubled contract made is worth four times the normal trick score, plus the usual 50 points "for the insult." Thus any redoubled contract scores a game, except one club or one diamond redoubled.

If you surpass yourself and make more tricks than you have contracted for when doubled or redoubled, each extra trick (or overtrick) is worth what your opponents would have gotten if you had gone one down. Suppose you are doubled in three hearts when you are vulnerable and make eleven tricks. You score as follows: 180 (i.e. 90 + 90) for three hearts doubled, plus 500 for a vulnerable game, plus 400 (200 + 200) for the two overtricks, plus 50 "for the insult." The total is 1130.

Slam Bonuses

For bidding and making a small slam (twelve tricks) you score 500 if not vulnerable, and 750 if vulnerable. These bonuses are doubled for a grand slam, but remember that grand slams should very rarely be bid. If you bid a grand slam and go one down, you have lost not only the points for tricks and the bonus for a small slam which you could have had, but the value of a game as well.

Honors

If you hold all the aces in a no-trump contract, you get a bonus of 150. You get a similar bonus of 150 for having all the five top trumps (ace, king, queen, jack and ten), and a bonus of 100 for having any four of the five top trumps. To score these bonuses, all the cards that matter must be in the same hand. (Honors do not count in duplicate scoring.)

♣

Scoring

A score-pad consists of tall narrow pieces of paper with a line printed down the middle and across the middle. Your scores go on the left, your opponents' scores on the right. All scores should be entered as close as possible to the central horizontal line. It is usual to write a large X at the top of the pad, to keep track of the dealer. If your left-hand opponent deals at the beginning, write "1" in the left-hand quadrant. When your partner deals the second hand, write "2" in the top quadrant and so on.

Points for contracts bid and made go below the line, i.e. the horizontal line. All other scores, for bonuses and penalties, go above the line. When either partnership scores a game, draw a horizontal line below the score across both columns.

Example:

14

(we)	(they)
50	
300	
500	90
360	40

On the first deal, you deal with nobody vulnerable, your opponents bid one notrump and make ten tricks. They score 40 for the trick they bid, a part-score that goes below the line, and 90 for the three extra tricks above the line.

On the second deal, with the opponents vulnerable, you bid six hearts, are doubled and make twelve tricks for your contract. You score 360 (180 + 180) below the line and draw a line below it, eliminating your opponents part-score. You also score above the line: 500 for the non-vulnerable slam; 300 for the non-vulnerable game; and 50 for making a doubled contract.

If play ended at this point you would win by 1080, worth $5.50 to each of you at a stake of half a cent a point. However, you have two deals remaining. Both sides now start from zero for the next deal for the purposes of scoring a game.

♦

Rubber Bridge

In this traditional form of the game, play continues indefinitely until one partnership has scored two games. When that happens, the winners of the rubber score 700 (if they have scored two games without reply) or 500 (if their opponents already have a game).

Four-Deal Bridge

In the popular four-deal variety of the game, you keep the same partner for four deals and then cut again to decide which of the other players you will have next as your partner. Each deal is slightly different, in a way that is explained later.

At the end of four deals the net score for the winners is rounded to the nearest 100 (50 counts as 100) and if it has been agreed to play for a stake the losers pay up. For example, if your stake is half a cent (and it might be much less or much more). A net profit of $970 wins you $5. At that stake it would be rare to win or lose more than $20 in an evening.

Four deals will normally last about half an hour.

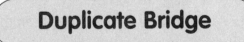

Duplicate Bridge

Keep each card in front of you, face down, as it is played, instead of throwing the card in the middle of the table to form part of a trick. At the end of the deal your thirteen cards go into the appropriate pocket of a tray (called a "board") which then goes to another table to be played there. Each deal is scored separately. A part-score is worth 50. Game bonuses are as in four-deal bridge: 300 for a non-vulnerable game; 500 for a vulnerable game.

♣

Quiz

1. What is the highest possible bid at bridge?
   If you succeed at this contract, what would you score
   (a) below the line? (b) above the line?
2. Both sides are vulnerable, and you bid four spades,
   which is doubled? If you make (a) nine tricks, (b)
   ten tricks, (c) eleven tricks how many points are
   scored, and where do they go on the score-pad?
3. You bid three clubs and make ten tricks. What is
   the lowest bid on the next hand that will get you a
   game?
4. You are South and bid one no-trump. Your partner
   bids three no-trump, which becomes the contract.
   (a) Who is the declarer? (b) Who is the dummy?
   (c) Who makes the first lead? (d) Who shuffled
   the spare deck?

16

Quiz Answers

1. Seven no-trump. (a) 220. (b) 1300 not vulnerable
   (1000 + 300) or 2000 vulnerable (1500 + 500).
2. (a) 200 above the line to the opponents.
   (b) On your side, 240 below the line, plus 500 for the vulnerable
   game and 50 for the insult above the line.
   (c) As (b) with an extra 200 above the line for the overtrick.
3. One no-trump. (Forty points are needed, and two clubs or two
   diamonds would also score this amount.)
4. (a) You, South, are the declarer. (b) Your partner, North, is the dummy.
   (c) Your left-handed opponent, West, makes the first lead. (d) Your
   partner, North, shuffled the spare deck while you were dealing.

♦

Chapter 3

The Basis of Bidding

Valuation

Almost all bridge-players use a simple point-count to value their hands:

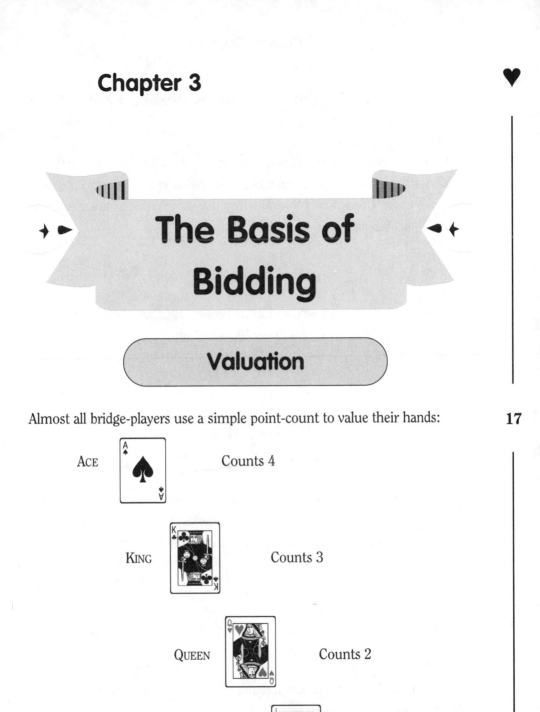

Ace   Counts 4

King   Counts 3

Queen   Counts 2

Jack   <u>Counts 1</u>

♣

This gives a total of 10 points in each suit, and 40 points in the deck. If your side is to take more than its share of the tricks, you will normally need more than your share of the high cards.

When you have sorted your hand into suits (it is convenient to have the red and black suits alternating) the first step is to count your high-card points. It sometimes saves a little effort to remember that an ace, king, queen and jack together total 10 points:

♠ A J x x *   ♡ K Q x   ◇ 10 x x   ♣ A Q x

If you mentally fit the spade and heart honors together, they add up to 10, now add the club ace-queen (4 + 2) giving a total of 16.

After a little practice you will find that you can count your high-card points very quickly.

Distribution

The high cards form only part of the strength of a bridge hand. Almost equally important is the way the cards are divided between the four suits. This is the "distribution," "shape" or "pattern" of the hand. Consider these four hands:

(a) ♠ J x x   (b) ♠ J x   (c) ♠ K J x x x (d) ♠ K J x x x x
    ♡ Q x x   ♡ Q x x   ♡ x x   ♡ x
    ◇ K x x   ◇ K x x   ◇ x   ◇ —
    ♣ A x x x   ♣ A x x x x   ♣ A Q x x x   ♣ A Q x x x x

All these hands have 10 points in high cards, but they all have different "shapes." To describe the shape of a hand, bridge-players list the lengths of the suits, starting with the longest.

Hand (a) is 4-3-3-3   Hand (b) is 5-3-3-2
Hand (c) is 5-5-2-1   Hand (d) is 6-6-1-0

* Note that throughout this book, and in other bridge books, an "x" indicates any small card below the ten.

Whenever you look at a bridge hand make a conscious note of the shape as well as of the high-card points. Do this when the dummy is exposed to view just as much as for your own hand. After a time you will find that you are fully aware of all the common shapes, and this awareness is a great asset when playing or defending a hand.

Clearly it is an advantage to have a long suit which you can nominate as the trump suit. It is also an advantage, if you are going to play in a trump suit, to be short in a side-suit (i.e. a suit which is not going to be trump): the shortage limits the number of tricks you can lose quickly in that suit, and gives you extra chances in the play.

Good players make allowances for the shape of their hand. They bid conservatively with a "shapeless" hand, such as example (a), and bid freely when they have a lot of shape, as in (c) and (d).

The inexperienced player needs a guide to help value the shape of his hand. Several methods have been published, but the suggestion in the next section is recommended as an improvement on all previous formulae. It will help the reader to select bids which will correspond closely with expert practice.

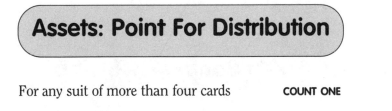

Assets: Point For Distribution

For any suit of more than four cards	**COUNT ONE**
For any singleton (suit with one card) unless it is king, queen or jack	**COUNT ONE**
For any void (suit with no cards)	**COUNT TWO**

These distributional points are called assets. As in real life these may decline or increase in value, according to changing circumstances.

The total of your high-card points and your assets will normally determine your bidding action. If the total is 13 or more, provided you have at least 10 in high cards, you can open the bidding at the one-level.

♠

♣ The following is a table of common patterns, showing the assets they each have:

4-3-3-3; 4-4-3-2	= 0 assets
4-4-4-1; 5-3-3-2; 5-4-2-2; 6-3-2-2	= 1 asset
5-4-3-1; 6-3-3-1; 6-4-2-1	= 2 assets
5-4-4-0; 5-5-2-1; 6-4-3-0	= 3 assets

As an exercise the reader should extend this table to include other distributions

Choice Of A Trump Suit

The more the merrier is the general rule in choosing a trump suit. Remember that you have a partner, and that it is your combined length that counts.

If you and your partner have eight cards between you in any suit, then your opponents have only five cards in it. Eight-five is a good working majority, so any suit in which you and your partner have eight or more cards will be a good trump suit. Anything less is likely to prove unsatisfactory. Seven trumps in the partnership hands may be acceptable on rare occasions. To play with less than seven trumps is foolish because the opponents will have the majority. Something has surely gone wrong with the bidding.

20

Assets Boom And Slump

An eight-card fit is regarded as normal, and your assets do not change in value. but if you can judge that your combined trump fit is better than eight cards your assets boom as follows:

With a nine-card fit	assets DOUBLE
With a ten-card fit	assets TRIPLE
and so on	

But if the bidding suggests that the partnership does not even have a normal fit, assets slump and become worthless. But they could conceivably revive. We shall see examples of this later. It is important to note that this revaluing procedure applies to both members of the partnership.

A Caution

Remember that very few bridge players consciously count points for shape, although the better ones bid as though they do. Any conversation at the card-table refers to high-card points only, and if your partner asks you how many points you had in your hand do not include your asset points when answering.

How Far To Bid

If you can calculate that you and your partner between you hold:

25 points or less	stop in a part-score
26-32 points	bid a game
33 or more	bid a slam

We shall see in later chapters what your partner's bids show in points, and from that how to judge the prospects of making a game or a slam. But at this point we can usefully list a few general rules.

(i) If at any stage in the bidding you feel sure that your side has less than 26 points, then stop in a part-score. Usually this means that you must pass partner's last bid, whatever it was; occasionally it is possible to transfer to a better part-score, but only do this if you are sure partner will not keep on bidding.

(ii) If during the bidding you judge that a game is possible but not certain, make a further bid below the game level. If you can calculate that your combined hands hold 23 or 24 points at least, then you can consider that game is likely: try to make an *encouraging* bid, which will urge your partner to go to game if he has any strength in reserve. Two no-trump is almost always an encouraging bid and so are certain suit bids which take the bidding one short of game – there will be several examples in later chapters.

(iii) If during the bidding you judge that game is certain, because you can count 26 points in the combined hands, you must ensure reaching a game contract.

If you know that you have between you eight cards at least in a major suit, bid game in the major suit.

If a combined eight-card major suit is impossible or improbable, you should usually bid three no-trump.

On rare occasions bid to game in a minor suit: three no-trump is usually easier to make. Five clubs or five diamonds may be the indicated contract if the combined hands have ten or more cards in the suit; or if three no-trump is impossible because the opponents have bid a suit which your side cannot guard.

If you are sure of game, but cannot be sure what game to bid, then make a bid below the game level which you are sure your partner will not pass. When you know you have the strength for a game, *never* make a bid below game which your partner might pass.

(iv) If you hope the combined hands may have the 33 points needed for a slam, try to encourage your partner to bid to slam. The most obvious way of doing this is to make a bid above game, but below the slam level.

(v) If you feel sure of a slam, either bid it directly or make a lower bid which you are sure your partner will not pass.

The essential rule in this section can be put slightly differently and is worth emphasizing:

Look for a combined eight-card major suit. If you find it, that will be the right denomination. If you cannot find one, and wish to be in game, usually bid three notrump.

22

Bidding A Suit

The general rule is that bidding a suit shows at least four cards in that suit. The hope is that partner will also have four cards, so that a good trump suit is discovered. In some situations (as we shall see later) a bid of a suit guarantees a five-card suit, and if partner has three-card support he knows a good fit has been found.

Do not worry about the strength of a suit; in choosing a trump suit it is the length that matters. Some bridge books used to lay down that certain suits were biddable and other weaker suits were not; but nowadays this distinction can be almost completely disregarded. A suit containing **5-4-3-2** can be bid just as much as a suit of **A-K-Q-J**.

Some Refinements

(1) In borderline situations, count your aces and tens. If you have several, bid aggressively; if not, bid cautiously.

(2) Remember that it is an advantage in attack to have high cards in your long suits:

		(b)	
(a)	♠ A K Q x x		♠ x x x x x
	♡ A x x x		♡ x x x x
	◇ x x x		◇ A K Q
	♣ x		♣ A

Both these hands count to 15, with 13 in high cards and 2 assets. But a good player will bid much more aggressively on hand (a) than hand (b). This is partly because (a) is better in attack, and partly because (b) is better in defense. For example, if clubs are trump, hand (a) is quite likely to be worth only two tricks, while hand (b) should certainly take three and perhaps four.

♣

(3) A singleton king, queen or jack does not count as an asset because it is not worth its full high-card weight. However, when revaluing a hand with a fine fit you can, if you wish, count it as a small singleton. When your assets triple, a singleton Jack can count as 3 assets instead of 1 high-card point.

(4) If you plan to play notrump, count a long suit as an asset but do *not* count short-suit assets.

Quiz

1.   How many points are there in the following hands, counting both points for high cards and points for assets?

(a) ♠ K J x
♡ A Q x
◇ K Q 10 x x
♣ A K

(b) ♠ A Q x x x
♡ A J x x
◇ x x x
♣ J

(c) ♠ A x x x x
♡ —
◇ x x
♣ A Q x x x x

24

2.   What should the final contract be on the following pair of hands, and what is the combined point count?

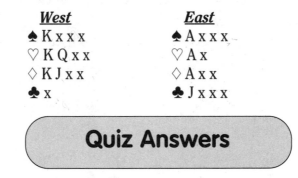

West	*East*
♠ K x x x	♠ A x x x
♡ K Q x x	♡ A x
◇ K J x x	◇ A x x
♣ x	♣ J x x x

Quiz Answers

1.   (a) 23 points (22 for high cards + 1 for an asset).
(b) 13 points (12 for high cards + 1 for an asset, since a singleton jack is not an asset).
(c) 14 points (10 for high cards + 4 for assets).

♦

2.   Four spades. The combined hands have eight cards in this major suit, and total 26 points, including 1 asset in the West hand.

Chapter 4

Notrump Bidding

One Notrump Opening Bid

Nearly all bids at bridge fall into two classes: limited and unlimited. Limited bids give a clear picture of the bidder's hand, and leave the major decisions to partner, who can visualize the combined holdings. Unlimited bids are vague exploring efforts, seeking more information about partner's hand.

An excellent example of a limited bid is a bid of one no-trump. It is an exact bid, describing both the type of the hand and the strength of the hand:

(i) The hand must be balanced, suitable for no-trump.
     The shape must be:

          4-3-3-3
     or   4-4-3-2
     or   5-3-3-2 with the five-card suit a minor.

♣

(ii) The hand must have 15, 16 or 17 points.[1] It is most important that hands of any other strength should not bid one no-trump. The following are typical examples for the bid:

(a) ♠ A Q x x
♡ K J x
◇ A J x
♣ Q x x

(b) ♠ A x x x
♡ A Q
◇ Q x x
♣ Q J x x

(c) ♠ A x x
♡ A Q
◇ Q x x
♣ Q J x x x

Note that example (c) has 16 points, counting the asset for the long club suit. A partner of conservative bridge habits might complain about this, and expect 16 high-card points; if so, it would be best for the sake of partnership harmony to pretend you miscalculated your points.

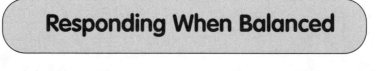

Responding When Balanced

26

If your partner opens one no-trump, and your own hand is reasonably suited to notrump, the correct action is a matter of simple arithmetic:

(a) ♠ K x x
♡ J x x
◇ x x x x
♣ A x x

(b) ♠ K J x
♡ J x x
◇ 10 x x x
♣ A x x

(c) ♠ K x x
♡ x x
◇ 10 x x x x
♣ A K x

Pass is correct with hand (a). With 8 points opposite a maximum of 17 there cannot be 26 points in the combined hands. When you are sure there is no game possible, then stop. Any balanced hand with from 0 up to 7 points should say pass.

Two notrump is correct with hand (b). With 9 or 10 points game is possible but not certain, so an encouraging bid is made urging partner on if he has a little extra. The opener will go on to three no-trump unless he has a minimum.

[1] This is the usual modern range. The traditional range, now rarely used, was 16, 17, or 18. In that case, the responses shown below become one point weaker. Discuss this with an unfamiliar partner.

◆

Three notrump is correct with hand (c), because there must be at least 26 points in the combined hand, counting a point for the asset in diamonds. Three no-trump fixes the final contract, and the opening bidder will pass automatically. Here, as usual, the decision is taken by the partner of the player who makes the limited bid.

With an even stronger hand, consider six notrump. With a balanced hand and 16-17 points, bid four no-trump, an invitation for the opener to bid six. With 18-19 points, bid six no-trump directly.

Three notrump would also be the right bid holding 10 points or more and a long suit, if the long suit is a minor:

♠ J
♡ x x x
♢ x x x
♣ A K J x x x

You should nearly always prefer three notrump to five of a minor suit. Here your clubs will be very useful to your partner in three notrump; he will probably make six tricks in the suit.

27

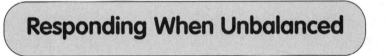

Responding When Unbalanced

In bridge terminology "unbalanced" has nothing to do with mental instability. It means a hand unsuited to no-trump play, i.e. a hand with a shape which would not qualify for a one no-trump opening bid.

If game is impossible, i.e. when you are holding less than 8 points, bid two of a suit which has at least five cards:

(a)   ♠ x x x x x x   (b)   ♠ A x x x x
            ♡ x   ♡ x x
            ♢ x x x   ♢ Q x x x
            ♣ x x x   ♣ x x

♣

Bid two spades with either of these hands, fixing the contract. The opening bidder must now say "pass," and accept his partner's decision that there is no chance of game.

In each case, two spades should prove a better contract than one no-trump. Hand (a) would be quite useless in a no-trump contract, but will take two or three tricks if spades are trump. Hand (b), with 7 points opposite at least 16, can expect to make two spades: seven trumps in the combined hands are certain, and eight are likely.

If game is certain, bid three spades or three hearts if you have a five-card suit:

(a)   ♠ K x x x x   (b)   ♠ A x x
           ♡ x x   ♡ A J x x x
           ◇ A x x x   ◇ —
           ♣ Q x   ♣ A 10 x x x

28

With hand (a) bid three spades, which asks the opener to choose between four spades and three no-trump. If he has only two cards in spades he will bid three notrump, but with three or four cards he will support to four spades. Whichever he does, you will pass.

With hand (b) bid three hearts, asking partner to choose between hearts and notrump. But holding 17 points (13 for high cards + 4 for assets; an eight-card suit is guaranteed in at least one suit) we can be sure of the 33 points needed for a slam; remember that the opener must have at least 16. So, whatever the opener does we shall follow up with a bid of six clubs, and let him choose between hearts and clubs as a trump suit. He will give you a preference to six hearts unless he has more clubs than hearts.

Note that a bid of three diamonds or three clubs* over one notrump in itself hints at a slam. As we have seen, if the responder holds a minor suit and is only interested in a game, he simply bids three notrump.

If you can see that the right contract is four of a major suit, simply bid it:

           ♠ A K J x x x
           ♡ x x x
           ◇ x x x
           ♣ x

◆

Bid four spades. This must be the right contract, because you can count eight spades in the combined hands, and you can count 26 points. A good general rule in bidding is this: if you know where you are going, bid what you think you can make.

Transfer Bids

The previous section describes the traditional method. However, many modern players, particularly in duplicate, use transfer bids. A two-diamond response to one notrump shows at least five hearts and almost any strength. The opening bidder automatically bids two hearts and partner reveals his strength: he passes if he is weak, bids two notrump or three hearts to invite game, or forces another bid from opener by bidding a new suit.

Similarly, a response of two hearts shows at least five spades and forces the opener to bid that suit. A response of two spades shows a hand with length in the minor suits.

One of the purposes of this is to make the weaker hand the dummy. It is an advantage for the opening lead to come around to the strong hand.

Transfer bids also operate following an opening bid of two notrump.

Responding Two Clubs

(The Stayman Convention)

Virtually all bridge-players use a response of two clubs to one notrump artificially. It is called Stayman, and the idea is simple. The bid asks opener the question: "Have you a four-card major suit?"

If the opener has a four-card major suit he bids it, bidding two hearts if he happens to hold four cards in both hearts and spades. If the opener has no four-card major suit, he bids two diamonds.

♣   The convention is very valuable on hands on which the responder feels that a major suit may be the best spot in which to play the hand:

    (a)   ♠ A J x x   (b) ♠ A x x x   (c) ♠ A x x x x
          ♡ x   ♡ x   ♡ x x
          ◇ K 10 x x   ◇ K x x x   ◇ K x x x
          ♣ Q x x x   ♣ J x x x   ♣ J x

    Hand (a), with 11 points, is sure of a game. The bid is two clubs, hoping for a bid of two spades which would be raised to four spades. Over two diamonds the second bid by responder will be three no-trump which will probably end the bidding. However, if the opening bidder has four cards in both majors, the bidding will follow this sequence:

Opener	*Responder*
1 NT	2 ♣
2 ♡	3 NT
4 ♠	

    After three notrump the opener knows his partner has spades, for if he had neither major suit he would have bid three notrump at his first turn.

    Hand (b), with 9 points, hopes for a game but is not quite certain. The bid is again two clubs, intending to raise two spades to three spades and otherwise to bid two notrump on the next round of bidding. Both sequences are encouraging, and the opener will go on to game unless he has a minimum.

    There are several refinements of the convention, but there is only one other important point. If the two-club bid is followed on the next round by three clubs, the opener must pass. The responder announces a weak hand with a long club suit and a strong preference for clubs as against notrump. (Discuss this with an unfamiliar partner, who may think differently.)

Two-Notrump Opening Bid

This shows a balanced hand with 21 or 22 points. Usually it shows an orthodox notrump shape, as for one notrump (4-3-3-3 or 4-4-3-2 or 5-3-3-2), but the shape requirements are not quite as rigid as for a one-no-trump bid. (Discuss this with an unfamiliar partner, who may think differently.)

The following are typical examples:

(a) ♠ A Q x x   (b) ♠ A x x   (c) ♠ A x
     ♡ K J x   ♡ A Q   ♡ A Q
     ◇ A J x   ◇ K x x   ◇ Q J x
     ♣ A Q x   ♣ A Q J x x   ♣ A Q J x x x

All these hands count 21, counting assets, and should bid two no-trump. Hand (c) has a slightly unusual shape, but the long club suit will be very useful in no-trump, and partner can still rely on at least two-card support for any suit he chooses to bid.

31

Responding To Two Notrump

With less than 5 points, say "pass." It is true that with 4 points there might just be a game (22 + 4 = 26), but when nearly all the points are in one hand it pays to be conservative.

With from 5-10 points and no interest in a major suit, bid three notrump.

With 11 points bid four notrump, an encouraging bid inviting the opener to bid six notrump if he has 22 points. (Four notrump over one notrump invites six no-trump in a similar way, and shows 16 points.)

With 12, 13 or 14 points bid six notrump, because the combined hands must have 33 points.

Suit bids in response to two notrump bear a close resemblance to the same responses to one notrump, except that there are no weak bids available; any bid promises that a game will be reached.

The following examples cover the main possibilities:

(a) ♠ K x x x x
    ♡ x x
    ♢ J x x x
    ♣ x x

(b) ♠ K x x x x x
    ♡ x x
    ♢ x x x x
    ♣ x

(c) ♠ K x x
    ♡ J x x x
    ♢ x
    ♣ 10 x x x

With hand (a) bid three spades, inviting the opener to choose between four spades and three notrump. If he has only a doubleton spade he will bid three notrump.

With hand (b) bid four spades, fixing the contract in the same way that four spades over one notrump does.

With hand (c) bid three clubs. This is an artificial bid very like two clubs over one notrump, and is used mainly to find out whether the opener has a four-card major suit.(But players using transfer bids, described above, would respond three hearts with (a) or (b), showing length in spades.)

Quiz

♥

1. On which of the following hands would you open with a bid of one notrump?

(a) ♠ K x   ♡ Q J x   ◇ A J x x x   ♣ K J x
(b) ♠ A Q x   ♡ K Q x   ◇ A J x   ♣ K x x
(c) ♠ x x   ♡ A Q x x   ◇ A J x   ♣ K Q J x
(d) ♠ K x   ♡ A Q x x   ◇ A x   ♣ Q J x x x
(e) ♠ A J x x x   ♡ Q J x   ◇ K x   ♣ A J x

2. If your partner opens one no-trump, what would you bid with each of the following hands?

(a) ♠ K x x   ♡ Q x x x   ◇ x x   ♣ Q x x x
(b) ♠ —   ♡ A Q J 10 x x   ◇ 10 x x x   ♣ J x x
(c) ♠ x   ♡ Q x x   ◇ A x x x x   ♣ Q x x x
(d) ♠ Q x x   ♡ A x x x x   ◇ Q x x x   ♣ Q
(e) ♠ Q x x   ♡ A x x   ◇ Q J x x x   ♣ J x
(f) ♠ x x x   ♡ Q x x x x   ◇ K x x x   ♣ x
(g) ♠ Q x x   ♡ A x x x x   ◇ J x x x   ♣ x
(h) ♠ A Q x x   ♡ K J x   ◇ A K x   ♣ Q x x

33

3. What would be the best bidding on the following pairs of hands? West is the dealer in each case.

(a)

West	East
♠ A J x x	♠ K x
♡ A J x x	♡ K x x
◇ Q J x	◇ K x x x
♣ K J	♣ 10 x x x

(b)

West	East
♠ A J x x	♠ K x x x
♡ A J x x	♡ K x x
◇ Q J x	◇ K x
♣ K J	♣ 10 x x x

4. If your partner opens two notrump, what would you bid with these hands?

(a)   x x   A x x x x   10 x x x x   x
       x x   A x x x   10 x x x x   x x

♠

Quiz Answers

1.   (a) and (c) only. (b) is too strong with 19 points, and (d) is not a notrump shape. One spade, with a five-card major is orthodox with (e) but one notrump is not unreasonable.

2.   (a) Pass. (b) Four hearts (the hand has 11 points). (c) Two notrump (not ideal for notrump but this is the only likely game – the long-suit asset counts, but not the short-suit asset, so the hand is worth 9 points). (d) Three hearts (unless using transfer bids). (e) Three notrump (the long-suit asset counts). (f) Two hearts (unless using transfer bids). (g) Two clubs, followed by a minimum bid in hearts. However, a two-heart bid by partner can be raised to game, since your two assets have doubled. (h) Six notrump.

3.

(a) West	East	(b) West	East
1 NT	2 NT	1 NT	2 ♣
3 NT	Pass	2 ♡	2 NT
		4 ♠	Pass

4.   (a) Three hearts (unless using transfer bids). (b) Three clubs (Stayman), hoping for a heart fit.

Chapter 5

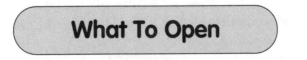

Suit Openings & Responses

When To Open

Always open with 13 points.
Never open with less than 13.

Thirteen is half the 26 points needed for a game, which is no coincidence. If you and your partner both pass with 12 points, no great harm is done because no game was possible; but if you both pass with 13, you have missed a game – a bridge tragedy.

But do not open one if you have less than 10 high-card points and a lot of assets. Some hands like these qualify for a higher-level opening described in Chapter Seven.

What To Open

The vast majority of bridge hands are opened with a bid of one of a suit. One club, one diamond, one heart, or one spade shows a minimum of 13 points and usually a maximum of 20 points – but some hands with 21-23 points are opened with a one-bid.

♣   Care is needed in choosing the right suit to bid. If we choose the wrong suit our next bid, as we shall see in Chapter Six, may be an impossible one. Bridge books generally give a lot of examples without any comprehensive conclusions: this book will reverse the process.

The modern rule* is:

A major-suit opening promises   FIVE cards or more

A minor-suit opening promises   THREE cards or more

Within this limitation there are two guidelines:

1.   BID THE LONGEST SUIT
2.   With suits of equal length,
            BID THE HIGHER-RANKING SUIT

There is one minor exception. With three diamonds and three clubs, bid one club.

36

Remember that the strength of the suit is unimportant.

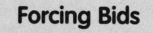

Forcing Bids

If you are confident that the right contract is three no-trump, or four hearts or four spades, it is simple enough to bid it. But frequently you may feel confident of a game, but unsure of the right denomination. You must then explore the situation and extract information from your partner by making a forcing bid which your partner is not allowed to pass.

Forcing bids after an opening one-bid in a suit are of two kinds:

I.   *Game-forcing bids.* These guarantee that the combined hands have at least the 26 points needed for a game; both players must therefore continue at least until a game is reached.

---

* An opening bid in a strong four-card major suit is an acceptable alternative, adopted by many but not recommended for inexperienced players.

There are three main situations in which a bid is game-forcing: ♥

(i)   Any jump bid by the responder in a new suit, skipping exactly one level.* For example:

Opener	**Responder**
1♠	3♣

This is not only guarantees a game, but hints at a slam. (Some tournament players, however, use this as a weak bid by partnership agreement.)

(ii) A jump bid in an unbid suit by the opener:

Opener	*Responder*
1 ♣	1 ♡
2 ♠	

(iii) Almost all bids following a game invitation: **37**

Opener	*Responder*
1 ◇	1 ♠
3 ◇	3 ♠

II. *One-round-forcing bids*. Certain bids carry this message: "I may have a hand on which game is certain, so please make at least one more bid."

There is one major rule:

(i) ***Any bid of a new suit by the responding hand is forcing for one round***:

Opener	*Responder*	*Opener*	*Responder*	*Opener*	*Responder*
1 ♣	1 ♡	1 ♡	2 ♣	1 ♣	1 ♠
				2 ♣	2 ♡

♠

* Traditionally, any jump bid in a suit, whether or not already bid, was forcing. A few people still play this way.

♣

But this does not apply if responder passed originally:

Responder	Opener
Pass	1 ♡
2 ◇	

Nor if the preceding bid was one notrump:

Opener	Responder
1 ♣	1 ♠
1 NT	2 ♡

And there are two specific situations in which a new suit by the opener is a one-round force:

(ii)   After a fit has been found:

Opener	Responder
1 ♠	2 ♠
3 ◇	

38

(iii) After a two-level response:

Opener	Responder
1 ♠	2 ♣
2 ♡	

Remember that bids in notrump or in a suit already bid by the partnership are seldom forcing. The only important exceptions is a jump response of two notrump. Here are two special cases:

Opener	Responder	Opener	Responder
1 ♡	2 ♣	1 ♡	2 ♣
3 ♡		2 NT	3 ♡

The responder has showed strength with his response, and in neither case would it be logical to stop short of game.

♦

Limited Responses

If your partner bids, for example, one heart he shows between 13 and 20 points. With 6 points or more you must therefore bid because there is a chance of a game: always make a bid if your combined hands might have 26 points. If possible, it is advisable to make one of the limited, descriptive bids in the following table:

Point-count	GAME PROSPECTS	BID WITH HEART SUPPORT	BID WITH BALANCED HAND
0-5	Nil	Pass	Pass
6-9	Poor	Two hearts	One notrump
10-12	Promising	Three hearts	Waiting bid in new suit
13-15	Certain	Waiting bid in new suit	Two notrump

(It is assumed that partner has bid one heart.)

Consider the following hand:

♠ x x   ♡ K x x x   ◇ K x x x   ♣ x x x

Over one heart the bid is two hearts (usually showing four-card support in hearts, but can sometimes be made with three-card support). But if the opening bid had been one spade the response would be one notrump, which usually shows a hand with fewer than three cards in partner' suit.

These two responses of two hearts and one notrump are both *discouraging*, and signal to partner that game is *unlikely*.

A jump response promises four-card support. A jump to the four-level would show a hand with less than 11 high-card points, only able to bid game because the assets have boomed:

♠ x   ♡ J x x x x   ◇ x x x x x x   ♣ x

♣   If partner opened one spade you would have to pass. With a likely misfit your assets are worthless. But if he bids one heart, indicating a ten-card fit, your four assets triple in value and your total worth is 13. This is an extreme case of assets booming. Usually a raise to four will show a hand with 6-10 high-card points that has been improved by the fit.

A response of three notrump is better than a response of two notrump and about equivalent to an opening one-notrump bid.

It will be seen that the table does not provide for hands in the 10-12 point range. The usual solution is to make a waiting bid in another suit, but a 10-point hand may be treated as 9, and a 12-point hand may be treated as 13.

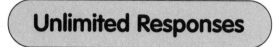

Unlimited Responses

A one-over-one bid, such as one heart over partner's one-club bid, shows a point range of 6-15, or perhaps even more. But a two-over-one bid, such as two clubs over partner's one heart shows a point range of 11-15 or perhaps even more; 6-9 points is too weak to make a forcing bid at the level of two.*

As with opening bids, there may be a problem in selecting the right suit.

There are three simple rules:

(i)   Bid the longest suit.

(ii)   With two five-card suits, bid the higher-ranking.

(iii)   With two or three four-card suits, bid the suit which keeps the bidding as low as possible.

♠ x x   ♡ A K x x x   ◇ x   ♣ K 10 x x x

In this hand the suit to bid is hearts because it is higher-ranking. Over one diamond, bid one heart; over one spade, bid two hearts.

♠ x x   ♡ A J x x   ◇ Q J x   ♣ K 10 x x

---

* Most serious tournament players do this somewhat differently. A two-level response in a suit shows 13 points or more and is (virtually) forcing to game. As a corollary, a 1NT response is forcing and is used with many hands in the 10-12 point range.

40

But with four-card suits, we must try to keep the bidding low. Over one diamond, bid one heart, but over one spade, bid two clubs.

There are one or two special points to note. Firstly, always bid a major suit in preference to supporting partner's minor suit:

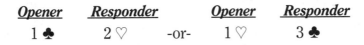

♠ A J x x   ♡ x x x   ◇ x x ♣ Q x x x

If partner bids one club, bid one spade rather than two clubs. Always look for a fit in a major suit, because game in a major suit is far more likely than game in a minor suit.

Secondly, if partner bids one spade, a bid of two hearts takes the bidding high quickly, and should only be made with a five-card or longer suit. With only a four-card heart suit there is always a better bid than two hearts.

With 16 points or more, and a substantial suit, make a single jump bid in a new suit, e.g.

Opener	*Responder*		*Opener*	*Responder*
1 ♣	2 ♡	-or-	1 ♡	3 ♣

These responses, skipping one level, guarantee a game and hint at a slam. Select the suit, if in doubt, in exactly the same way as for a minimum suit bid.

Assets Slump

If partner opens in a suit in which you have a singleton or void, a misfit is likely and your assets slump. Count assets as worthless until, perhaps, a fit is found later in the auction. Similarly, if you open the bidding and partner responds in a suit in which you have a singleton or a void, your assets slump and are worth zero.

♣

1. You were the dealer, and it is your bid. What call would you make with each of the following hands?

(a)	♠ A K Q J	♡ J x	◇ x x	♣ x x x x x
(b)	♠ A K Q J	♡ J x x	◇ x	♣ x x x x x
(c)	♠ A K Q J x	♡ J x	◇ x	♣ x x x x x
(d)	♠ J x	♡ x x x x x	◇ A K Q J x	♣ x
(e)	♠ A J x x x	♡ —	◇ A J x x x	♣ x x x
(f)	♠ A J x	♡ A x x x	◇ A x x x	♣ x x
(g)	♠ A x	♡ A x x x	◇ A x x x	♣ A J x
(h)	♠ K J x x	♡ x	◇ K J x x	♣ K J x x
(i)	♠ A x x x	♡ A x x x	◇ A J x	♣ x x
(j)	♠ A x x x	♡ A J x	◇ x x	♣ A x x x
(k)	♠ A x x x	♡ A J x	◇ A x x	♣ x x x

42

2. What would you respond with each of the following hands if your partner had opened (i) one club, (ii) one heart or (iii) one spade? (Three answers required for each hand.)

(a)	♠ x	♡ Q x x x	◇ K x x x x	♣ x x x
(b)	♠ J x x	♡ x	◇ K x x x x	♣ Q x x x
(c)	♠ J x	♡ K x x x	◇ K x x x	♣ Q 10 x x
(d)	♠ J x	♡ A Q x x	◇ Q x x	♣ J x x
(e)	♠ K x x x	♡ A J x x x	◇ x	♣ J x x
(f)	♠ x	♡ A J x x x	◇ K Q x x x	♣ x x
(g)	♠ K J x	♡ Q 10 x	◇ A x x	♣ K 10 x x
(h)	♠ A K J x x	♡ x	◇ x x	♣ A Q x x x
(i)	♠ A J x x	♡ K Q x x	◇ K x	♣ A x x
(j)	♠ x	♡ A K Q J 10 x	◇ x x x	♣ A x x

♦

Quiz Answers

♥

1. (a)Pass; only 12 points. (b) one club; 13 points, and clubs the longest suit. (c) one spade. (d) one heart. (e) one spade. (f) one diamond. (g) one notrump. (h) one diamond. (i) one diamond. (j) one club. (k) one club.

2. (a) (i) One diamond, (ii) Two hearts. (iii) Pass. (With a shortage in spades, six high-card points are needed to respond.)
    (b) (i) Two clubs, (one diamond acceptable). (ii) One notrump.
    (iii) Two spades.
    (c) (i) One diamond, (one heart acceptable).. (ii) Two hearts.
    (iii) One notrump.
    (d) (i) One heart. (ii) Three hearts. (iii) Two clubs. The last is a waiting bid with an 11-point hand, since no accurate descriptive bid is available.
    (e) (i) One heart. (ii) Four hearts. (iii) Four spades.
    (f) (i) One heart. (ii) Four hearts. (Better still, three spades, a splinter bid. (See page 69.) (iii) Two hearts.
    (g) (i), (ii), and (iii) Two notrump.
    (h) (i) Two spades. (ii) One spade. (iii) Three clubs.
    (i) (i) One heart or two hearts. (ii) Two spades. (iii) Three hearts.
    (j) (i) Two hearts. (ii) Three clubs. When no second suit exists to jump in, we must invent one. (Better still, bid three spades. See page 69.)
    (iii) Two hearts. As we are short in spades, we cannot count this as 16 points for a forcing jump bid.

43

♠

The following hands are all "normal" opening bids with 13-16 points, and on all of them a suitable weak rebid has to be found:

(i) ♠ K x x x ♡ K x ◇ A x x x x ♣ K x

When your partner responds one spade to one diamond, you bid *two spades*. You show at least three-card and probably four-card support for spades.

(ii) ♠ K x ♡ K x x ◇ A x x x x ♣ K x x

Now your rebid is *one notrump*, showing a balanced hand and 13-15 points. (A balanced hand with 16 points would presumably have bid one notrump originally.)

(iii) ♠ K x ♡ x x ◇ A x x x x ♣ A Q x x

Now the rebid is *two clubs*, showing an unbalanced hand probably with five diamonds and four or five clubs. In rare cases the opener might have 17 or even 18 points, but his partner will assume a normal 13-16.

(iv) ♠ K x ♡ x x ◇ A J x x x x ♣ A x x

Now the rebid is *two diamonds*, normally showing a six-card diamond suit. (A player who bids a suit twice without any indication of support, almost invariably has at least six cards in his suit.)

The next group of hands comprise the strong opening bids with 17-18 points. With such hands the opener must try to make a strong, encouraging rebid, promising partner a combined holding of at least 23 points.

(v) ♠ K J x x ♡ x ◇ A K x x x ♣ A x x

With four-card spade support, spades must be the contract, and the bid is *three spades*. (The hand counts 17 points, including 2 for assets.)

(vi) ♠ x x ♡ K Q x ◇ A K J x ♣ A Q x x

Chapter 6

Rebids

After A Limited Response

If the opener has no interest in game he will pass if the response was a single raise (e.g. 1 ♡ – 2 ♡).

But if the response was one notrump, the opener may dislike notrump and wish to play a part-score in a suit. The following sequences are both unconstructive, and assets are not counted because a misfit is likely:

(a) 1 ♡   1 NT   Shows maximum of 16 and a six-card suit. Partner
    2 ♡   must pass.

(b) 1 ♡   1 NT   Shows maximum of 17, with at least five hearts and at
    2 ◇   least four diamonds. Partner usually passes or gives a
                    preference to two hearts, but he might raise to three
                    diamonds invitationally.

If there has been a discouraging response (1♡ -2♡ , or 1♡ – 1 NT each showing 6-9 points) the opener may then feel that game is possible but not certain. If he has 17 or 18 points, he knows that the combined hands have a minimum of 23 points, and tries to make one of the following encouraging bids:

♣

(a) 1♡   1 NT
    2 NT

Shows 17-18 and a balanced hand with a five-card heart suit. With 8 or 9 partner bids 3 NT, or 3♡ if he has three-card heart support. With 6 or 7 only, he passes or shows a six-card minor suit.

(b) 1♡   1 NT
    3♡

Shows 17-18 and at least a six-card heart suit. Partner raises to 4♡ with 8 or 9 points and two or three cards in hearts. Otherwise with 8 or 9 he may bid 3 NT. With weaker hands, he should pass.

(c) 1♡   2♡
    3♡

Shows 17-18, probably with 6 hearts. Partner passes with 6 or 7 but bids 4 with 8 or 9.

(d) 1♡   2♡
    2 NT

Shows 17-18 and a balanced hand. (An unlikely bid on normal methods.) Partner with 8 or 9 bids 4 or 3 NT, but with 6 or 7 he bids 3 or passes.

(e) 1♡   2♡
    3♢

Shows 17-18, and urges partner to bid 4 hearts. If in doubt he should be guided by his diamonds: strength or shortage is very desirable. If not strong enough to bid 4♡, he must bid simply 3♡ .

If the opener can judge that game is certain or almost certain, he will usually bid a game directly. The following sequences, for example, almost always end the auction:

(a) 1♡   1 NT
    3 NT

Shows 19-20 and a balanced hand.

(b) 1♡   1 NT
    4♡

Shows 19+ and at least six hearts.

(c) 1♡   2♡
    4♡

Shows 19+ including assets.

(d) 1♡   2 NT
    3 NT

Shows a balanced hand, probably less than a 1 NT opening.

♦

(e) 1♡   3♡
    4♡

No interest in slam

♣

But sometimes the opener will need to explore:

(f) 1♡   2♡
    3 NT

Shows 19-20 and a balanced hand. Partner reverts to 4♡ unless his hand is balanced as well.

(g) 1♡   1 NT
    3♣

Shows 19+ and an unbalanced hand with hearts and clubs. Guarantees a game.

After A Suit Response

The last section was concerned with opener's action when partner had made a limited, descriptive bid. Although there are a lot of possibilities, the action required is a matter of common sense, and detailed examples are not needed. The reader need not try to memorize the sequences given in the last section, but should be content with trying to grasp the general principles.

But if you bid a suit and your partner responds in another suit, there are then many possibilities. Each player can have one of a wide range of hands, varying greatly in type and strength. The responder has asked for more information about the opener's hand, and the opener must therefore select a rebid which will describe both his strength and his shape.

Suppose that your opening bid was one diamond, showing 13-20 points, or even more, and that your partner bid one spade, showing 6 -15 or even more. You may not pass, because your partner has asked you to describe your hand and may be very strong.

You must first decide into which of the following strength categories your hand falls:

13-16	normal opening bid	make a weak rebid
17-18	strong opening bid	make a strong rebid
19-20 or even more	very strong opening bid	make a game rebid.

♠

This time opener rebids *two notrump*, showing a balanced hand with 20 points, slightly too good for a 1 NT opening (15-17) but not good enough for a 2 NT opening (21-22).

(vii)   ♠ K x   ♡ A Q x x   ◇ A K J x x   ♣ x x

Two hearts is now correct. A normal hand with hearts and diamonds would bid hearts first, so this sequence shows more diamonds than hearts, *and* a strong hand. This is a reverse bid, and it is important to be able to recognize such a bid. If you bid two suits in such a way that if your partner wishes to return to your first suit his bid will be at the three level, your second bid is a reverse and therefore strong. Other examples would be:

Opener	*Responder*	*Opener*	*Responder*
1♡	2♣	1♠	2◇
2♠		3♣	

(viii)   ♠ K x x   ♡ A x   ◇ A K Q x x x   ♣ x x

Now the rebid is *three diamonds*, showing at least a six-card diamond suit.

Lastly come a group of very strong opening bids, in which the opener has 19 or 20. With such hands he is virtually certain of making a game when his partner has shown a minimum of 6 points, and he must therefore make either a direct game bid, or make a bid which guarantees a game.

(ix)   ♠ A K x x   ♡ x x   ◇ A K J x x   ♣ K x

Four spades is now correct. With an assured combined eight-card spade holding a game is practically certain, and it would be overly timid to bid only three spades, which partner may pass.

(x)   ♠ K x   ♡ A K J x ◇ A K J x x ♣ x x
(xi)   ♠ K x   ♡ x x   ◇ A K J x x ♣ A K J x

Three hearts on (x) and *three clubs* on (xi) are correct. Both bids are single jump bids in a new suit, and therefore guarantee a game.

♣

Misfits - A Reminder

Here we must issue the usual caution about misfitting hands. In making your rebid you must not count any points for assets if you have fewer than two cards in partner's suit.

♠ —   ♡ A Q x x   ◇ A K x x x x   ♣ K J x

You open one diamond, holding 20 points (17 for high cards +3 for assets). If your partner bids one heart or two clubs, your hand is worth full value, and you can make a game rebid: over one heart, *four hearts*, and over two clubs, *three hearts* (forcing). (Better still, three spades. See page 69).

But if partner bids one spade, the hand looks like a complete misfit. With a void in spades, we may not count any points at all for assets. Our hand is worth 17 points only, and we are content to make a strong reverse rebid of two hearts.

50

Table of Rebids

The rebids discussed above can be tabulated as follows:

	TYPE OF HAND			
STRENGTH OF HAND	*Support for partner (usually 4-card)*	*balanced (for NT)*	*two-suited*	*one-suited*
Normal opening 13-16 points	2 ♠ (May be 3 cards)	1 NT (usually 13-14)	2 ♣	2 ◇
Strong opening 17-18 points z	3 ♠	2 NT (18, since 17 would open 1 NT)	2 ♡	3 ◇
Very strong opening,19-20 points	4 ♠	2 NT * (often 18)	3 ♡ or 3 ♣	—†

(Assuming again an opening of one diamond with 13-20 points, and a response of one spade, showing 6-15 points.)

♦

If Partner Has Bid At The Two-Level

If you open one heart and your partner bids two clubs he has shown 10-15 points or even more. You therefore need only 16 points to be sure of a game, and the following game-forcing rebids are available: 2 ♠; 3 ◊; 3 ♡ and 4 ♣. Minimum bids are likely to show minimum hands (2 ♥; 2 NT; 3 ♣) but remember that a new suit in this position (2 ◊) is a one-round force, often artificially, and partner will not pass.

---

* — 3 NT is a rare specialized rebid, showing long, solid diamonds and stoppers in the unbid suits.
† — a bid of four diamonds hardly exists since it rules out 3 NT. But 1 ♡ - 1 ♠ - 4 ♡ is common.

Preference Bids

If your partner bids two suits he is asking you to choose between them. Suppose you have:

♠ K J x x x   ♡ Q x   ◇ x x x   ♣ x x x

Your partner bids one diamond, and you have just enough with 7 points, including one asset to bid one spade. He now bids two clubs, which is a minimum rebid. Your first instinct is to say "pass," but you should think again. Remember you need as many trumps as possible, so try to decide which is your side's longest combined suit. If your partner's suits are of equal length it will not matter. He cannot have more clubs than diamonds, for he would then have opened with one club, but he may well have more diamonds than clubs. So you must bid two diamonds, which is a simple preference bid showing no extra strength at all.

If your partner bids two suits, you may only pass with more cards in his second suit than his first. If you want to pass, but have equal length in his two suits, always give him a preference to his first suit in case that is longer.

Sign-Off Bids

If your partner at some point bids notrump, and you simply bid your own suit again at the lowest level, this is a clear warning: you have no further ambitions, and he is required to pass. There are two obvious cases, one of which we have had already:

(a)	*Opener*	*Responder*	(b)	*Opener*	*Responder*
	1 ♠	1 NT		1 ◇	1 ♠
	2 ♠			1 NT	2 ♠

In each case the player with spades must have at least a six-card suit, and in each case his partner must now pass. (Similar in principle is 1 NT – 2 ♣; but not 2 NT – 3 ♣, which is a new suit at the three-level and therefore forcing.)

52

Essentially similar is a rebid of your own suit when your partner has bid two suits, e.g.

Opener	Responder
1 ◇	1 ♠
2 ♣	2 ♠

Again you must have at least a six-card suit, and see no prospect of a game.

How Responder Encourages

If at this second turn the responder sees no hope of a game, he usually passes. He may occasionally make a preference bid or a sign-off bid as described in the last two sections, and these actions show no extra strength at all, and are equivalent to passing.

If the opener has made a weak rebid, almost any other bid the responder may make short of game is an encouraging bid. It would be impossible to catalogue them all, but the following are representative samples:

Opener	Responder		Opener	Responder
(i) 1◇	1♠	(ii)	1 ◇	1♠
2♠	3♠ or 2 NT		1 NT	2 NT
	or 3♣ or			
	3 ◇ or 3 ♡			

Opener	Responder		Opener	Responder
(iii) 1◇	1♠	(iv)	1 ◇	1♠
2♣	2 NT or 3 ♣		2 ◇	2♡ or 2 NT or 3◇
	or 3◇			

All the various fourth bids shown indicate about 11 or 12 points and urge the opener on to game. When the bid is a new suit by the responder, it is forcing and he may well have more than 11 or 12.

♣   There are a few special cases to note:

(a) 1 ♠ 2 ◇
    2 ♡ 3 ♠   Shows exactly three cards in spades – with more the support would have been immediate. It would be nonforcing if he had passed originally.

(b) 1 ◇ 1 ♠
    2 ♣ 2 ♡   This, and any similar sequence in which the first four bids are minimum bids in different suits, is a bid of the "fourth suit". Most experts regard this as a forcing bid, often based on a worthless holding in the suit bid. If the responder really had hearts, he would probably bid notrump, so 2 ♡ may be a useful expedient if he wants to bid notrump but is weak in hearts. This is a point to discuss with your regular partner.

(c) 1♣ 1♡
    1♠ 2 ♠

54
(d) 1♣ 1♡
    1♠ 1 NT   These are both hybrid bids, which are mildly encouraging. They usually show 8-10 points.

Rebidding A Suit

A point made above should be emphasized. Unless partner has indicated some support, rebid your first suit only when it contains six cards or more. With only a five-card suit, find some other bid. This applies to both the opener and the responder.

What's the deal?

♦

Jumps By The Responder

This is a gray area and must be discussed with your partner. Such bids are always forcing in a new suit, and are invitational, not forcing, when the jump bidder passed originally.

Otherwise there are two schools of thought. For the traditionalist, all such bids are forcing. For the modernist they are all invitational, encouraging but not forcing.

The following are examples:

	Opener	*Responder*		*Opener*	*Responder*
(i)	1♠	3♠	(ii)	1♣	1♡
				1♠ 3♠	
(iii)	1♣	1♡	(iv)	1♣	1♡
	1♠	3♣		1♠	2 NT

So with a new partner it is very important to ask this question: "Are jump bids by the responder forcing or invitational?"

Quiz

1. What do you rebid with each of the following hands if you have opened the bidding with one club and your partner has replied (i) one heart, (ii) one spade, (iii) two clubs or (iv) two notrump. Four answers to each part are required.)

(a)	♠ J x	♡ x x	◇ A x x	♣ A Q J x x x
(b)	♠ A x x	♡ x x	◇ Q x x	♣ A Q x x x
(c)	♠ A x x x	♡ x	◇ J x x	♣ A Q x x x
(d)	♠ A x x x	♡ x	◇ A J x	♣ A Q x x x
(e)	♠ A K x x	♡ —	◇ A x x x	♣ A J x x x
(f)	♠ K x	♡ x x	◇ A K J x	♣ A Q x x x
(g)	♠ A Q	♡ K J x	◇ K x x	♣ A Q x x x
(h)	♠ A x	♡ K Q	◇ x x x	♣ A K x x x x

55

♣

2. In each of the following bidding sequences your partner has just made the last bid. In each case say how many points you think he has and state whether the bid is weak, encouraging or forcing.

	Opener	*Responder*		*Opener*	*Responder*
(a)	1 ♣	1 ♡	(b)	1 ♡	2 ♢
	2 ♠			2 NT	
(c)	1 ♣	1 ♡	(d)	1 ♡	3 ♡
	1 ♠	3 ♠		4 ♢	
(e)	1 ♡	2 ♣	(f)	1 ♡	2 ♣
	2 ♢	2 ♡		2 ♢	3 ♡
(g)	1 ♡	1 ♠	(h)	1 ♡	1 ♠
	1 NT	3 ♠		2 NT	3 ♠

Quiz Answers

1. (a) (i) Two clubs. (ii) Two clubs. (iii) Pass. (iv) Three notrump.

    (b) (i) One notrump. (ii) Two spades. (iii) Pass. (iv) Three notrump.

    (c) (i) One spade. (ii) Two spades. (iii) Pass (iv) This is difficult. Three clubs is the least evil.

    (d) (i) One spade. (ii) Three spades. (iii) Pass. The point count justifies an effort with two spades, but prospects of eleven tricks with clubs as trump are very poor. (iv) Three notrump.

    (e) (i) One spade. (ii) Four spades. (Better still, four hearts – a splinter bid. See page 69.) (iii) Two diamonds, to be followed by a spade bid, but two spades is acceptable. (iv) Three diamonds, to be followed by a spade bid.

    (f) (i) Two notrump or two diamonds. (ii) Two diamonds. (iii) Two diamonds. (iv) Three diamonds.

    (g) (i) Two notrump. (ii) Two notrump. (iii) Three notrump. (iv) Six notrump.

    (h) (i) Three clubs. (ii) Three clubs. (iii) Two notrump or three clubs. Even three notrump is a plausible gamble. (iv) Three notrump or three clubs.

♦

♥

2.   (a) 19-20, or even more, forcing

(b) 13-15 or even more, discouraging.

(c) 13-15, forcing in the traditional style. 10-12, invitational in the modern style. Shows four-card spade support.

(d) 17-20, forcing. (A cue-bid, showing the diamond ace and suggesting a six-heart slam contract. See page 68.)

(e) 10-12, a preference bid.

(f) 13+, forcing. (Jump preference, shows three-card heart support.)

(g) 13 or more, forcing in the traditional style. 10-12, invitational in the modern style. Shows six or more spades.

(h) 6+, forcing. Shows a six-card suit.

57

♠

Chapter 7

Bids of More Than One

Traditional or Modern

Before World War II it was standard to open a very powerful hand with two of the longest suit. This guaranteed a game contract, and the negative response with a weak hand was two notrump.

This method is still used occasionally in family rubber bridge, but it has been completely abandoned by good players. We recommend the modern style, in which all powerful hands are opened with two clubs.

Opening Two Clubs

With any hand containing 23 points or more, including assets, bid two clubs. This is an entirely artificial bid, the "two clubs" convention, which is used by almost all experienced players.

Two clubs simply shows a very powerful hand, certain or almost certain of a game.

♠

(No promise is made about the holding in the club suit, which could be a void. Clubs is chosen for the conventional bid because it is the lowest-ranking suit.)

The following are typical opening bids of two clubs:

(i)	♠ A K Q x x	♡ A K x x x	◇ A x	♣ x
(ii)	♠ A x x	♡ A K Q J x x	◇ A K x	♣ x
(iii)	♠ A Q x	♡ A K J x	◇ A Q J	♣ K Q x
(iv)	♠ A Q x	♡ A K J x	◇ A J x	♣ K Q x

If partner has an ace and a king or better, he makes a positive response in his longest suit (but if his suit is diamonds, he must bid *three diamonds*). If he has 8 points or more and a balanced hand he bids two notrump. In either case the bidding progresses happily and naturally at least to a game and usually to a slam.

But four times out of five, if your partner can bid two clubs showing an enormous hand, your cards will be at the best feeble and at the worst abysmal. Suppose you have:

♠ 10 x x   ♡ 10 x x   ◇ 10 x x x   ♣ 10 x x

The bid is *two diamonds*. This is a conventional negative bid, quite unrelated to diamonds, showing you have fewer than 7 or 8 points.

After an opening bid of two clubs the bidding *must* continue to game (except, as we shall see, in one special situation).

Let us see how the bidding develops if our sample two-diamond response sits opposite our four sample two-club bids.

If the opener has hand (i), the bidding goes:

2 ♣	2 ◇
2 ♠	2 NT
3 ♡	3 ♠
4 ♠	Pass

♥

Two diamonds is a conventional negative, and two notrump is virtually a second negative: responder *cannot* pass. Three spades is a preference bid, showing that responder's spades are at least as long as his hearts. The opener has thus been able to bid both his suits at a low level without any fear that his partner will pass short of game.

If the opener has hand (ii), the bidding goes:

2 ♣	2 ◇
3 ♡	4 ♡
Pass	

Two hearts instead of three hearts would be forcing, so three hearts announces a solid heart suit (i.e. containing all the top cards). By bidding four hearts the responder does his reluctant duty and continues to game.

If the opener has hand (iii), the bidding goes:

2 ♣	2 ◇
3 NT	Pass

By bidding three notrump the opener announces a balanced hand with about the values for a game: 25, 26 or 27 points.

If the opener has hand (iv), the bidding goes:

2 ♣	2 ◇
2 NT	Pass

Two notrump shows a balanced hand with 23 or 24 points. To raise to three notrump responder needs at least 2 or 3 points. With a worthless hand it is logical for responder to pass two notrump; this is the only situation after a two-club bid in which the bidding can die short of game.

♠

The Weak Two-Bid

A bid of two spades, two hearts or two diamonds shows a strong six-card suit and a moderate hand not strong enough in high cards to open with a one-bid. Each of the following hands would bid two spades:

(i) ♠ K Q J x x x   ♡ A x x   ◇ x   ♣ x x x

(ii) ♠ Q J 10 x x x   ♡ K x x   ◇ x   ♣ x x x

The high-card points are usually between 6 and 11. These hands are respectively a maximum and a minimum.

Responses to a weak two-bid are:

(a) Pass. Any hand short in opener's suit and with no interest in game.

(b) A single raise (2♠ -3♠). A moderate hand with a few spades but no interest in game. The raise is made solely to disrupt enemy communications. Opener must pass.

(c) A double raise (2♠ -4♠). Either a strong hand that expects to score game or a moderate hand with several cards in opener's suit. In the latter case the opponents can probably make a game in their suit, and we give them as much trouble as possible.

(d) Two notrump. Asks opener to define his hand. He rebids three of his suit with a minimum. With a maximum he bids a side-suit in which he has some strength, or 3 NT if his suit is solid.

(e) New suit bids are natural. They can be forcing or non-forcing by partnership agreement.

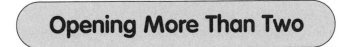

Opening More Than Two

Opening bids of three or more in a suit are known as pre-emptive bids.

The object of such bids is to annoy the opponents, and they are made on hands with a long suit and little or no outside strength. Suppose you have this hand:

♠ **K Q J** 10 x x x x   ♡ x   ♡ x x   ♣ x x

This hand is very useful if spades are trump, but practically valueless in any other contract. With such a hand, therefore, it pays to bid as many spades as you can afford as quickly as possible. If your partner has a few high cards all will be well; and if not, the opponents, with good hands, will have to start bidding at a high level, and are quite likely to miss their best contract.

How many spades you can afford to bid depends partly on vulnerability. You are half-expecting to be doubled and go down, so you must be more cautious if you are vulnerable, because the penalties for going down are larger.

Count your probable tricks. The hand above has clearly seven. Then:

> *if not vulnerable, add three tricks.*
> *if vulnerable, add two tricks.*

Then if the answer comes to nine or more, make the corresponding bid. So the above hand should bid four spades if not vulnerable, and three spades if vulnerable. These are the classical rules for making pre-emptive bids, but they are rather conservative. If you apply them strictly you will never lose more than a penalty of 500 points, which is roughly the value of the game your opponents could probably have made. but few good players apply them strictly, and you will get more fun out of the game if you apply them with a generous dash of optimism. Sometimes this may cause you to suffer a loss of 700, or 800, or even 900, but even this may be a hidden profit; sometimes the opponents, left to themselves, would have been able to bid and make a slam.

♣

Do not make pre-emptive bids with a strong hand: it is unwise to open with three or more holding 13 or more high-card points. If your partner has a good hand, you may cause your side to miss a slam.

You can make pre-emptive bids with a long suit if one of the opponents opens the bidding. The qualifications for these bids are similar to those for opening pre-emptive bids.

1.   You are vulnerable. What would your opening bid be with each of the following hands?

(a) ♠ x   ♡ A K Q x x x   ◇ K x x   ♣ K x x
(b) ♠ x   ♡ A K Q x x x x x ◇ x x   ♣ x x
(c) ♠ A   ♡ A Q 10   ◇ A K Q 10 x x x   ♣ x x
(d) ♠ x   ♡ A Q 10   ◇ A K Q 10 x x x   ♣ x x

2.   You are vulnerable and hold the following hand:

♠ x x   ♡ K x x x   ◇ A Q x x x   ♣ x x

What should you bid if your partner opens, vulnerable, with (a) two clubs, (b) two spades, (c) three spades?

1.   (a) One heart. (b) Four hearts. (c) Two clubs. (d) One diamond.

2.   (a) Three diamonds. (b) Pass. (c) Pass. Your partner is already hoping for two tricks in your hand – about what you have got.

64

♦

Chapter 8

Slam Bidding

A partnership that contracts for twelve or thirteen tricks, a small slam or a grand slam, needs to be more scientific than it would have to be at lower levels. More information is needed, but luckily more bidding space is available. There are two main considerations.

One is total strength of the combined hands. Thirty-three points is usually enough for a small slam and thirty-seven for a grand slam, in each case including distribution assets.

The second consideration is quick losers. It would be foolish to bid a small slam if the opponents could immediately cash two aces, or an ace-king combination. And it would be even more foolish to bid a grand slam against which the opposition takes an ace, because you have lost the value of a small slam.

Slam-bidding procedures can be divided into four categories: direct action; the Blackwood convention; cue-bidding; and miscellaneous.

Direct Action

This is often appropriate when both hands are balanced. If your partner makes a descriptive notrump bid at any point, showing his strength within narrow limits, you can raise to six notrump if you know that the combined hands have the required 33 high-card points.

♣

For example:

1 NT (15-17)	6 NT (18-20)	or	2 NT (21-22)	6 NT (12-14)	or	1♣ 6 NT (20)	2 NT (13-15)
Total:	33-37		Total:	33-36		Total:	33-35
	(i)			(ii)		(iii)	

In all these situations, and in many similar ones, a slightly weaker hand than the one that jumped to slam would bid four notrump, a natural invitation to six notrump, and a slightly stronger hand would probably bid seven notrump.

An unbalanced hand will often bid a small slam directly. He must be sure that the combined strength is adequate, and that there is no danger of losing the first two tricks.

	You	*Partner*
♠ A Q x x x	1♠	3 ♠
♢ A K J x		
♢ A J x	6 ♠	Pass
♣ x		

Your partner's jump raise of three spades showed, in the modern style, a hand slightly short of an opening bid, roughly 10-12 points, including at least four cards in spades. A direct bid of six spades is entirely reasonable. The combined strength is sufficient, since your original assets have doubled on account of the known nine-card fit. $19 + 4 = 23$, so the combined hands have at least 33 points. You know that the opponents cannot take the first two tricks. The chance that a grand slam will be a sound contract is poor.

66

♦

Blackwood

♥

The world's most popular bidding convention was designed to allow a player to find out how many aces his partner holds. In almost all cases (the exceptions are natural slam invitations in notrump as in the preceding section) a bid of four notrump asks partner to announce the number of aces he owns by means of coded responses:

FIVE CLUBS	shows	no aces (or, very rarely, four aces)
FIVE DIAMONDS	shows	one ace
FIVE HEARTS	shows	two aces
FIVE SPADES	shows	three aces

This is all so simple that many players leap into Blackwood at the slightest provocation, enjoying a sense of power. Several words of caution are needed:

67

(1) Do not use Blackwood unless you are sure the combined hands have sufficient strength for slam. You are simply trying to guard against the danger of having two aces missing. If the response shows that the partnership has three or four aces, you must be willing to bid at least a small slam.

(2) Do not use Blackwood when holding a void suit. The ace of that suit will be of little value to you.

(3) Do not use Blackwood when holding an unbid suit in which you might lose the first two tricks.

(4) If the Blackwood bidder follows with a bid of five notrump he is asking for the number of kings his partner holds, with the same schedule of responses at the six-level. This implies interest in a grand slam, so do not bid five notrump unless the partnership is known to have all four aces.

♠

♣

A popular modern variation is called Roman Keycard Blackwood. The king of the intended trump suit is counted an extra ace, making five "keycards". A five-club response shows zero or three keycards. A five-diamond response shows one or four. A five-heart response shows two, but no queen of trumps. A five-space response shows two, plus the queen of trumps.

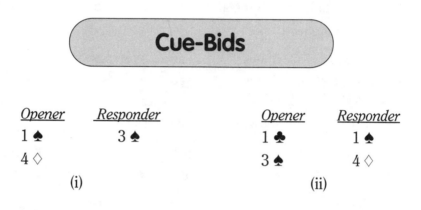

Cue-Bids

Opener	_Responder_		_Opener_	_Responder_
1 ♠	3 ♠		1 ♣	1 ♠
4 ◇			3 ♠	4 ◇
	(i)			(ii)

68

When the partnership is already committed to game and a fit in a suit has been found, a bid in some other suit is a cue-bid. This suggests a slam, and shows some control of the suit bid. This will usually be an ace, but might be a void, a king or a singleton.

The cue-bidder may be uncertain about the total strength of the partnership. Or he may have some feature that makes a Blackwood bid undesirable: a void suit, or an unbid suit with two quick losers. Partner may reject the slam suggestion by bidding the trump suit as cheaply as possible, make a cue-bid of his own, bid Blackwood, or bid a slam.

A modern term gaining favor is *control bid*. This leaves *cue-bid* for low-level bids in the opponent's suit. These usually show a desire to be in game but uncertainly about the choice of suit. see page 72, and page 75, example (vii)

Miscellaneous

There are three lesser slam bidding weapons that are popular among good players:

(1) *The Gerber Convention*. At any stage, a jump to four clubs from one notrump or two notrump asks about aces on the Blackwood principle. A response of four diamonds, for example, shows no aces or all four aces, four hearts shows one ace, etc. Gerber is needed because a bid of four notrump over one notrump or two notrump is a natural invitation to six notrump.

(2) *The Grand Slam Force*. When a suit fit has been found, a direct jump to five notrump, skipping past Blackwood, asks partner to bid a grand slam if he has two of the top three trump honors, ace-king, ace-queen or king-queen.

(3) *Splinter bids*. By partnership agreement, a jump to a meaningless level in a new suit announces a fit with partner's suit, interest in slam, and at most one card in the suit bid. For example:

Opener	*Responder*	or	*Opener*	*Responder*
1 ♠	4 ♣		1 ♣	1 ♠
			4 ◇	

69

Chapter 9

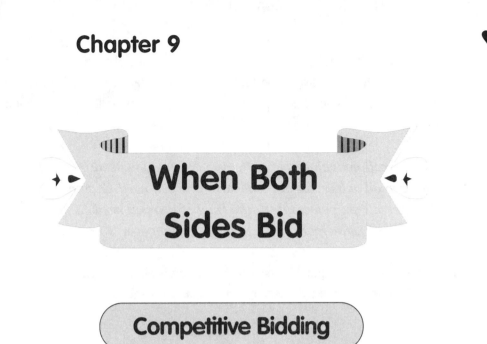

When Both Sides Bid

Competitive Bidding

Competitive bridge refers to the duplicate form of the game, in which each hand is preserved and played at least twice, and the prizes are master-points, trophies and prestige rather than cash.

But competitive bidding refers to the numerous situations in which both sides take part in the auction. Once both sides start bidding, myriad situations can arise in which delicate judgment is required. In the majority of these there is no substitute for experience: all that can be attempted in this book is to discuss a few common situations, and offer some general advice.

Simple Overcalls

If your right-hand opponent bids one of a suit and you want to make an overcall in your own suit, an essential requirement is a suit of at least five cards. If your side has opened the bidding, you can happily bid a four-card suit, but if the opponents take the initiative you must not bid anything less than a five-card suit.

---

* — An overcall is a bid made when the opposition have started the bidding. Do not confuse this, as some people do, with an overbid, which is a bid greater than the strength of your hand justifies.

♣

The strength required, including assets, is about that needed for an opening bid. There are two important factors to be taken into account: the vulnerability, and the level at which you have to bid. The following is a good rough guide:

> *To overcall not vulnerable at the level of one you need 10 points*
> *To overcall vulnerable at the level of one you need 13 points*
> *To overcall not vulnerable at the level of two you need 13 points*
> *To overcall vulnerable at the level of two you need 15 points*

These are minimum requirements. The maximum is about 18. The fourth case, vulnerable at the level of two, usually needs a six-card suit.

♠ x x   ♡ A K J x x   ◇ K Q x   ♣ x x x

72

This hand would justify a bid of one heart over one club at any vulnerability. Over one spade it would be worth two hearts not vulnerable, but an extra card in hearts would be needed to justify a vulnerable overcall.

If your partner makes an overcall you can bid your hand naturally. As you know he must have at least a five-card suit, you can support his suit happily with three cards, and at a pinch with a doubleton. If you are strong enough for game, you can usually bid it directly in his suit. But if you need to explore, you can jump in another suit, or bid the opponent's suit: this is a useful device in a lot of competitive situations, showing merely that you expect to get to game, but you are doubtful about what game. A bid of 2 NT, or a jump raise, e.g. from 1 to 3 , shows about 11-12 points, and is strongly encouraging. A bid of 1 NT, or a single raise, say from 1 to 2 , is mildly encouraging, while a suit-bid, e.g. 2 over 1 , is discouraging and suggests a weakish hand with a six-card or longer suit. With fewer than 9 or 10 points you should tend to pass the overcall as game is improbable.

♦

If your partner's opening bid is overcalled on your right, you should as far as possible ignore the overcall and bid as you would have done without it. If you bid one notrump, however, you should be rather stronger than usual, and hold 8-10 points with a stopper in the enemy suit.

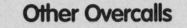

Other Overcalls

The meaning of a jump overcall (2 ♡ over an opposing 1 ♣, or 3 ♡ over 1 ♠) is a matter of style. The old style was to make this bid with a six-card suit and a hand too good for a simple overcall, perhaps 16-18 in high cards. But most good players nowadays use the jump as a weak pre-emptive action, roughly equivalent to a weak-two opening.

An overcall of one notrump shows a hand worth an opening notrump bid with a stopper in the enemy suit. An overcall of two notrump has no useful natural meaning and is used by good players to show considerable length in the two lower-ranking unbid suits. (Thus 1 ♡ , 2 NT would show length in clubs and diamonds.)

73

Pre-emptive overcalls we have already dealt with in Chapter Seven. This only leaves a resource which is so important that it needs a long section to itself.

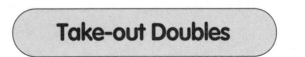

Take-out Doubles

Early in the history of bridge, players realized that a double of an opposing opening bid of one of a suit has negligible value as a penalty double.

So a double in this situation is used as a request to partner to bid one of the unbid suits. Suppose the player on your right bids one diamond and you have:

♠ A Q x x   ♡ K x x x   ◇ x   ♣ A x x x

♣   This is a very useful hand, provided a trump suit can be found, preferably a major suit in which your partner has at least four cards. So over one diamond you employ a double, asking your partner for information about his hand: it is called a take-out double.

    Almost always a take-out double guarantees at least three cards in each of the unbid suits, together with at least 13 points including assets. The following hands are minimum doubles of one diamond:

(a)	♠ A x x x x	♡ A x x x	◇ x	♣ K x x
(b)	♠ A J x x	♡ A x x x	◇ x	♣ K x x x
(c)	♠ A J x x	♡ A J x x	◇ x x	♣ K x x
(d)	♠ A Q x x	♡ A J x	◇ x x x	♣ K x x

    This last hand has 14 points, and its "flat" pattern is really better suited to defense. To attack with a double it is really desirable to have a shortage in the enemy suit.

    A double should be made with any hand of more than 18 points when no other bid seems suitable:

(e)	♠ A Q x x x	♡ K Q x	◇ J x	♣ A K x

    Whatever partner responds to your double, your next bid will be in spades.

    Now let us look at the other side of the picture. How does your partner respond to a take-out double?

(i)	♠ x x	♡ K x x x x	◇ x x x	♣ A x x
(ii)	♠ x x x	♡ x x x x	◇ x x x	♣ x x x

    One heart is the right bid on each of these hands if partner doubles one diamond. If you have (ii) and partner doubles one heart, you have to bid one spade and hope for the best; partner has asked for your longest suit other than hearts, so you must hide your misgivings and keep the bidding as low as you can.

(iii)	♠ x x	♡ K Q x x x	◇ x x x	♣ A x x

74

Two hearts, a single jump, is the bid if partner doubles one diamond and you have 9-11 points. This is encouraging but not forcing.

(iv) ♠ Q x x   ♡ x x x   ◇ A J x x   ♣ x x x

One notrump shows a stopper in the enemy suit, and 6-9 points – exactly the strength needed for a response of one notrump to a suit opening bid. Similarly, two notrump and three notrump would show 10-12 and 13-15, including at least one stopper and preferably two in the opponent's suit.

(v) ♠ x x   ♡ A K x x x x ◇ x x   ♣ A x x

Four hearts at once is now indicated over the double of one diamond. The values for a game are there, as you have an opening bid opposite an opening bid and partner has promised a fit in hearts by doubling.

(vi) ♠ x   ♡ x x   ◇ Q J 10 9 x x ♣ A x x x

75

Pass. With length and strength in the enemy suit the best plan is to make a penalty pass. The hand seems to be a misfit: it is unlikely that your side can make a game, but you can probably collect a good penalty by holding the opposition to four or five tricks in one diamond doubled. To make the most of the defense your partner should lead a trump.

You may have a problem opposite a double holding a game-going hand that needs to explore:

(vii) ♠ A Q x x   ♡ K x x x   ◇ A x x   ♣ x x

Two diamonds is the right bid, unexpected but logical. You cannot possibly want to play with diamonds as trumps: with length and strength in the enemy suit you would make a penalty pass as in the last example. Here and in other situations, a bid in the enemy suit announces to partner: "I am not sure where we are going, but I know we want to be at least in a game."

If it is your partner's opening bid that has been doubled on your right, the procedure is simple. With 10 points or more in high cards you redouble automatically, announcing to your partner that your side has the "balance of strength" – i.e. more than half the high-card strength in the deck. Often your best plan will be to double the opposition in whatever they choose to bid, and your partner will usually pass at his next turn in case you wish to double.

If you can raise your partner's bid over a double you should do so with a generous dash of optimism; and if you wish you can bid a long suit. In either case your partner will realize that you have less than 10 points.

Penalty Doubles

It is vitally important to distinguish between a take-out double, which asks you to bid another suit, and a penalty double, which asks you to pass in the expectation of beating the opposition contract.

A double of notrump is always for penalties. A double of a game bid is always for penalties. A double is always for penalties if your partner has made a bid.

So putting this the other way around, we can lay down that: a double is only for take-out if it is a double of a *low suit* bid when *partner has not bid*.

(a)	one heart	pass	pass double
(b)	one heart	pass	pass
	double		one spade
(c)	one heart	pass	two hearts	double double

These three doubles are all for take-out, asking partner to bid.

(d)	one heart	one spade	two diamonds double
(e)	four spades	double	
(f)	one notrump	double	

But these three doubles are all for penalties, and partner is expected to pass.

Profitable doubles often occur at a low level. Suppose you hold:

♠ A J x x x ♡ K J 9 x ◇ x ♣ A J x

Suppose that you open one spade and that your partner responds two diamonds. If your right-hand opponent overcalls with two hearts it would seem that he has made a mistake. Punish him with a penalty double. Your partner will nearly always pass, and you will score well.

A penalty double is attractive when you are short in your partner's suit. In general, you consider a penalty double when you know your side has most of the high cards. You should be eager to double when the opponents are vulnerable and you are not.

Three situations in which a penalty double should be considered are:

(i) Your partner opens with a suit and your right-hand opponent bids one notrump.

♣

(ii) Your partner opens with one notrump and your right-hand opponent overcalls in a suit.

(iii) You have opened the bidding, the second player has doubled and your partner has redoubled.

But be careful about a double when your partner has opened the bidding in a suit and the second player has overcalled. In this position almost all good players use a "negative double", meaning that the double is for take-out not penalties. Discuss this with an unfamiliar partner.

Redoubled contracts are very rare indeed; when they occur, one side or the other must be overly optimistic. The only common use for a redouble is, as we have seen, a good hand when your partner's opening bid has been doubled. In other low-level situations when your own or your partner's suit bid has been doubled for penalties, a redouble is a shriek for help, begging partner to bid something else.

Revaluing Your Hand

78

When both sides are bidding you frequently need to reassess your hand. When you have K J x in the opponent's suit, the value of your hand is considerably altered. If the player on your right has bid the suit, he probably has the ace and queen; your king and jack will be well placed in any contract, and if you hope to play in notrump you can count them as 6 points instead of 4. But if the player on your left has bid the suit, your king and jack are badly placed and worth very little.

Suppose the opponents have bid and supported a suit in which you have three or four cards. Your partner almost certainly has a singleton or a void, so if he is due to play the hand you can devalue the high cards you have in the enemy suit: the queen or jack you can write off completely, and even the ace is probably not worth its full value. On the other hand, you are entitled to be pleased if you hold three or four small cards, because your high cards in the other suits are almost sure to be useful to your partner.

♦

Quiz

1. If the player on your right bids one heart, what would you bid with each of the following hands?

(a) ♠ K x x x   ♡ A Q x   ◇ A x x x x   ♣ K x
(You are vulnerable.)

(b) ♠ K x x   ♡ A x x   ◇ A K x x x x   ♣ x
(You are vulnerable.)

(c) ♠ K x x x   ♡ x x   ◇ A K x x   ♣ A Q x
(You are not vulnerable.)

(d) ♠ K x x x x   ♡ x x   ◇ A Q x x   ♣ x x
(You are not vulnerable.)

(e) ♠ K x x x x   ♡ Q x x   ◇ A Q x x   ♣ x
(You are vulnerable.)

(f) ♠ x   ♡ K J x x   ◇ A Q x x   ♣ A Q x x
(You are vulnerable.)

2. The player on your left bids one heart, and your partner doubles. The next opponent says pass. What do you bid with each of the following?

(a) ♠ K x x x   ♡ x x x x   ◇ —   ♣ A x x x x
(b) ♠ x x x   ♡ x x x x   ◇ x x x   ♣ x x x
(c) ♠ K x x x   ♡ A J 9   ◇ x x   ♣ A J x x

79

♣

1. (a)　One notrump. (Much better than two diamonds.)

   (b)　Two diamonds.

   (c)　Double.

   (d)　One spade.

   (e)　Pass. (A borderline overcall of one spade. If the spade queen was held instead of the heart queen it would be worth it, but as it is the spade suit is thin, and the queen of hearts probably useless.)

   (f)　Pass. (With strength in the enemy suit it is usually best to keep quiet. Prospects are good in defense and poor in attack, as the hand is likely to be a misfit, so you should plan to defend.)

2. (a)　Two spades. (One spade would show nothing, so you must jump the bidding to show some values. Three clubs is not wrong, but game prospects are better in the major; when partner doubles one major suit, he usually has at least four cards in the other major suit.)

   (b)　One spade. (A horrible position. Your partner has forced you to bid, and you have no four-card suit available. All you can do is to bid your lowest three-card suit and hope for the best. Partner is likely to have a four-card spade suit.)

   (c)　Two hearts. (Bidding the enemy suit virtually guarantees a game. If partner bids two spades you raise to four spades, and otherwise you bid three notrump.)

♦

Chapter 10

The Elements of Play

Cashing A Suit

In this chapter we shall consider the management of a single suit. We shall assume that the contract is notrump, although of course the same basic principles apply in a trump contract.

If you have all the high cards in a suit in one hand there is no problem, but if the high cards are divided a little care is needed:

Declarer	*Dummy*
K J x	A Q x x

Declarer has the lead, and can make four tricks, for he has the four top cards available. If he leads a small card and wins with dummy's queen, he can then lead a small card and win the next two tricks with the king and the jack. But now the lead is the declarer's hand, the ace is left in dummy, and there may be no way of getting the lead there.

There is an easy way of avoiding this difficulty. When "cashing" a suit in which you have all the high cards,

play first the high cards from the shorter hand.

♣

So, in our example, declarer's first move should be to lead out his king and jack. He is then certain to end up where he wants to be– in the long hand. Try it and see.

The above combination is worth four tricks. If we added an extra small card to the dummy's holding it would be worth an extra trick, but if we added an extra small card to declarer's hand we should still make only four tricks.

Remember that the maximum number of tricks to be made from a suit is the number of cards in the longer hand.

The rule that you should play the high cards from the short hand applies equally well if the opponents have the ace, or the ace and king:

(a) _Declarer_   _Dummy_   **(b) _Declarer_   _Dummy_**
    Q x   K J x   J x   Q 10 9 x

In (a) the declarer must play his queen, planning to force out the ace and make two tricks quickly. In (b) he must lead his jack in order to force out the ace and king, and make two tricks more slowly.

82

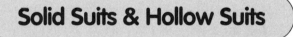

Strictly
speaking, a solid suit is one with a sequence of top cards, such as A K Q, or A K Q J. The length of the suit is the number of tricks to be had, and that is that. But we can regard as solid, in a sense, any sequence of high cards (i.e. touching in rank) whether headed by the ace or not:

(a) **K Q**   (b) **K Q J**   (c) **K Q J 10**

In each case the opponents are sure to make a trick with the ace so (a) is worth one trick, (b) is worth two tricks, and (c) is worth three tricks, after the ace has gone. The tricks you can make added to the trick or tricks the opposition can make add up to the length of the suit. Similarly:

♦

(d) **Q J 10**   (e) **Q J 10 9**   (f) **Q J 10 9 8**

In (d) you have a 3-card suit, and the opponents have the ace and king, so you have one trick. In (e) you have two tricks, and (f) three tricks.

If you have one of these solid suits, one of your opponents probably has a hollow suit, consisting of some small cards headed by the ace, or the ace and king. Take this example:

Declarer   *Dummy*

x x x   A K x x x

Now we must consider what the opponents hold. They have altogether five cards, and the most likely way for five cards to be divided is three cards in one hand and two in the other. (This is odds on, and will happen about two times in three.) If this is so, we can assume that one opponent has Q J 10 (any other three cards would be equivalent, so if the queen, jack and ten are divided in the opposing hands the situation is basically the same.) The Q J 10 we know is worth one trick, and dummy has a five-card length. The difference is four, so we should be able to make four tricks. You can check this by leading out the ace and king, which win, followed by a small card losing to the enemy queen. At this point dummy's two remaining small cards have been established as tricks – all the other cards in the suit have gone.

There could be a catch in this: we may not be able to get the lead into dummy to make tricks with the two established small cards. We can avoid this trap with ease by a maneuver known as ducking, or a duck.

When you are hoping to turn the small cards in a long suit into winners and the opponents have one or two certain tricks,

give the opponents their certain tricks as quickly as possible.

In the last example we know we must lose one trick, so we lose it at once; declarer leads a small card and plays another small card from dummy. Now when the lead is regained in either hand, the ace and king make the next two tricks and the lead is in dummy to make tricks with the established small cards.

♣

Here is a similar case:

Declarer	*Dummy*
x x x	A x x x x

The opponents have five cards, which we hope will divide 3-2. If so, one opponent can have K Q J, worth two tricks to him. If he has two tricks, and dummy has a five-card length, we should be able to make three tricks. As we must lose two tricks, we start by playing a low card from each hand; when we regain the lead, we "duck" again. Now the opponents have made their two tricks, and when we are back in the lead dummy's ace will collect their last card, and the lead is right to cash dummy's two remaining small cards.

In the last two examples we have in effect made a wish that the opposing cards should be divided 3-2. We can be optimistic about that, because the odds always favor an even break when an odd number of cards is missing.

But prospects are not nearly so good if the opposition have an even number of cards and you need an even break.

Suppose you have this combination:

Declarer	*Dummy*
x x	A K x x x

The opponents have six cards, so you make a wish that they will have three each. (This will happen about once in three times.) You must certainly lose one trick, so lose it at once: play a small card from each hand. If the enemy cards break 3-3 you can now make four tricks when you regain the lead. Your remaining small card may be most valuable to get the lead into dummy.

Declarer	*Dummy*
x x	A K Q x x

♦

Here again you wish for the opposing cards to split 3-3. If they do you can clearly make five tricks at once without trouble. If, as is more likely, they divide 4-2, you can lose a trick and hope later to make dummy's remaining small card. But it may sometimes happen that dummy cannot gain the lead in any other suit, and dummy's final "x" would then never make a trick. If declarer needs only four tricks from the suit, his best play may be to duck a trick at once by playing low from each hand. This is a simple example of the large family of "safety plays," in which a trick is surrendered, perhaps unnecessarily, to improve the overall chances of making the contract.

Broken Suits

The suit holdings discussed in the last section were clear-cut ones. We now move on to a wide range of scrappy holdings in which the prospects are harder to calculate. With solid suits and hollow suits it is of no importance which hand leads to the first trick. With broken suits the location of the first lead is quite vital. We now have a basic rule, applied consciously or unconsciously by all players past the beginner stage,

lead from low cards towards high cards.

First, here are three kindergarten positions:

Dummy has: K x   Q x x   A Q
                 (a)   (b)   (c)
Declarer has: x x   x x x   x x

In each case we must lead from declarer's hand towards the high cards. In (a) the ace is the vital card. If it is on the left we make a trick, and if not, we do not: a 50% chance. In (b) we make a wish for the ace and king to be on the left, and if the gods are as kind as that we can make a trick by leading twice towards the queen: a 25% chance. In (c) we must hope the king is on the left if we are

♣

to make two tricks. Lead a small card and put the queen on: another 50% chance. This is a "finesse"; there are many such positions, and some of them are rather complicated. Often it is necessary to lead twice towards the high cards:

Dummy has:	K Q x	K J 10	A Q J
	(a)	(b)	(c)
Declarer has:	x x x	x x x	x x x

In (a) we can make two tricks if the ace is on the left. In (b) we can make two tricks if the queen is on the left, by leading to the ten and then the jack. In (c) we can make three tricks if the king is on the left. In all three cases we must lead twice towards the high cards, and in each case we have a 50% chance. The next three cases are more complicated:

Dummy has:	A J 10	A Q 10	A J 9
	(a)	(b)	(c)
Declarer has:	x x x	x x x	x x x

86

In (a) we hope that the king or the queen or both are on the left, and we lead twice to the ten and then the jack. We shall make two tricks unless the king and queen are both on the right: a 75% chance.

In (b) we hope the king and jack are both on the left, in which case we make three tricks by leading first to the ten and later to the queen. But if the king and jack are both on the right, we make only one trick: another 25% chance. And if the opponents have one high card each, a 50% chance, we make two tricks. (c) is distinctly difficult. We could lead small to the jack, hoping for king and queen on the left, but this only a 25% chance. It is better to hope for the ten to be on the left, together with at least one higher card; lead a small card to the nine, and if this forces out the king or queen follow with a small card to the jack. This is in fact a 37½% chance: the figure is of little importance provided you remember the correct play.

high cards in both hands

Remember that the business of high cards is not merely to take tricks, but to kill the opposing high cards on their right. If we have only two or three high

♦

cards divided between the two hands, our aim must be to avoid having our high cards killed:

Dummy has:	Q x x	J x	Q J x x
	(a)	(b)	(c)
Declarer has:	A x x	A K x x	A x x

The principles are the same as in the last section: we have to hope that an opposition high card is favorably placed for us.

With (a) we hope the king is on the left, and lead small towards the queen. The ace is a sure trick anyway, and we have a 50% chance of a trick with the queen.

With (b) we want a trick with the jack, so we must hope that the queen is on the left and lead small towards the jack. This is another 50% chance.

(c) is often misplayed by quite good players. You should hope the king is on your left, and lead small to the jack. If this wins, come back to the ace and lead up to the queen. We now make three tricks if the king is on the left, or if the opposing cards split 3-3.*

But if the opponents hold only one or two high cards in the suit, the position changes completely. Instead of husbanding our high cards, and nervously hoping to grab a trick with a shaky-looking honor, we become killers. With the big battalions we are happy to sacrifice one of our lesser honor cards if we can kill an enemy high card in the process:

Dummy has:	A x x	K x x	A x x
	(a)	(b)	(c)
Declarer has:	Q J 10	J 10 9	J 10 9

With (a) we must try to prevent the enemy king taking a trick. This can only be managed if at some stage our ace kills the king, so we must hope the king is on the left (a 50% chance). Lead the queen and hope it is covered by the king. The ace will win and the jack and ten will be tricks. Whatever happens, do not play the ace until the king has appeared.

87

---

* — The advanced reader may spot a slight improvement here: it is fractionally better to play the ace first in case there is a singleton king on the right, but this is usually inconvenient as declarer needs an extra entry to his hand.

With (b) we can do nothing about the enemy ace, so we must try to catch the queen with our king. So hope the queen is on the left (a 50% chance) and

lead the jack, saving the king until the queen appears.

With (c) we must hope to kill either the king or the queen with the ace, so lead the jack and save the ace unless the king or queen appears. We have a 75% chance of making two tricks.

In these last examples we have been happily leading queens and jacks. But remember that this is seldom good policy. Normally you should lead a high card only if you are happy for an opponent to kill it, and this is rarely the case unless your side has at least four of the top six cards in a suit.

With a broken suit, and especially one shared between the two hands, it often helps if the opposition leads the suit for you:

Dummy has:	Q x x	K x x	A x x
	(a)	(b)	(c)
Declarer has:	J x x	J x x	J 10 x

With (a) and (b) we are by no means sure of a trick, but if we can delay playing the suit and persuade the opponents to lead it, then one trick is certain.

With (c) chances of making two tricks are very poor, but if the defenders lead the suit our prospects are excellent: we shall make two tricks provided the player who leads has at least one high card.

We have far from exhausted the possible combinations of high cards in the two hands. It is excellent practice for the inexperienced player to sort out one complete suit from a deck of cards, and deal out various combinations with different suit lengths. With practice of this kind it is soon possible to judge, when the dummy goes down, the prospects each suit offers. The declarer who can do this can then concentrate on the overall strategy of the hand, which we shall discuss in the next chapter.

Quiz

1. Which card would you lead in each of the following? (You may lead from either hand.)

Dummy has:	K Q J x	A x x	Q x
	(a)	(b)	(c)
Declarer has:	A x	Q x	A J 10 9

2. Say how many tricks you would hope to make with each of the following, and whether your chances of success are better or worse then even:

Dummy has:	A K x x x x	A x x x	A x x x
	(a)	(b)	(c)
Declarer has:	x x	K x x	x x x x

89

3. With the following combinations, say (i) how you would like the opposing high cards placed; (ii) how many tricks you would hope to make; and (iii) (optional, for amateur mathematicians) what your percentage chance is of making that number of tricks.

Dummy has:	Q 10 9	Q J x	A K 10
	(a)	(b)	(c)
Declarer has:	x x x	x x x	x x x
Dummy has:	K J x	A Q 9	K 10 x
	(d)	(e)	(f)
Declarer has:	x x x	x x x	x x x

Quiz Answers

1. (a) The ace (or a small card from dummy). (b) A small card from dummy. (c) The queen. (If a small card is played from dummy the queen is a nuisance, tending to block the suit.)

2. (a) Five tricks; better than even, one trick should be ducked, or given away, and then the king and ace played. (b) Three tricks; worse than even. One trick should be ducked, or given away, and then the king and ace played. (c) Two tricks; better than even. Two tricks should be ducked.

3. (a) (i) Jack on the left. (ii) One. (iii) 50%.
   (b) (i) Ace or king or both on left. (ii) One. (iii) 75%.
   (c) (i) Queen and jack on the left. (ii) Three. (iii) 25%.
   (d) (i) Ace and queen on the left. (ii) Two. (iii) 25%.
   (e) (i) King on left, or jack and ten on the left. (ii) Two. (iii) 62½%. (Lead small to the nine).
   (f) (i) Ace on left, or queen and jack both on the left. (ii) One. (iii) 62½%. (Lead small to the ten.)

Chapter 11

Playing The Dummy

Planning In Notrump

West	**East**
♠ A K Q 3	♠ 7 4
♡ K 6	♡ A 8 3
◇ K J 10 5	◇ 7 6 2
♣ Q 4 3	♣ K J 10 8 6

You are playing in three notrump, sitting West. North leads the queen of hearts and you inspect the dummy. At this point, before playing a card, you should try to make a plan.

The first step is to count your certain tricks. You have three spades and two hearts, totalling five. These tricks can wait: never be in a hurry to take your certain winners until you can count enough tricks for the contract.

You need nine tricks altogether, so four more must be developed; clearly these must come from the minor suits. The most promising place to develop extra tricks is usually your longest combined suit. Your longest combined suit

♠

♣

is clubs. As the clubs are solid after the ace, they should make four tricks. So we must play on clubs, because they will give us the extra four tricks we need. As soon as we can, we play the queen of clubs and carry on with the suit.

But there is another point to watch in the play of this hand – a point which demonstrates the importance of thinking before playing a card. If you want to assure making four club tricks you must save the ace of hearts as an entry to dummy and win the first trick with the king of hearts.

Entries

West	*East*
♠ A K Q 3	♠ 7 4
♡ A Q	♡ K J
◇ Q 10 8 6 2	◇ 9 5 4 3
♣ Q 4	♣ A J 10 9 6

Again you are playing three notrump as West. North leads the ten of hearts.

This time you have six sure winners, and need to develop three tricks. Your longest combined suit is diamonds, but a brief look shows that the diamond suit is useless: before any diamond tricks can be made, the defenders will have established at least three heart tricks. The club suit is a far better proposition, which should be worth four or possibly five tricks. If North has the king of clubs guarded once or twice we can kill it and make five tricks in clubs.

Your plan will be to lead the club queen and save the ace till the king appears. If the king appears on the first trick, life is easy. But if the defenders win a later club trick, it will be vital to get the lead back into dummy.

Dummy's only entry outside the club suit is the king of hearts. So you must be very careful at the first trick to play dummy's jack of hearts and then put the ace on it. Dummy's heart king is preserved as a safe entry card, to be used when king of clubs has been played and the clubs are established.

♥

Imagine that the hearts in the East and West hands are exchanged. Now you can win the first trick with heart king over dummy's queen, and save the ace as the entry for the clubs.

Entries are the essential lines of communication between the two hands, so never waste them. If you can win a trick in either hand, it will usually be better to win it in the strong hand, which probably has plenty of entries, and save the entry to the weak hand which may be very valuable later in the play. Consider the entry possibilities of the following:

Dummy has:

	(a)	(b)	(c)
	Q 8 3	K J 9	A 9 8 2
	A K J	A Q 10	7 6 4 3

With (a) you should normally win the first trick in the suit with the ace or king. Later you can if you wish get the lead into dummy by putting dummy's queen on your jack; or if it suits you better you can win two more tricks in your own hand. If you need the lead in dummy quickly, you can put dummy's queen on your jack at once. The one play that is utterly and hopelessly wrong is to win the first trick with the jack: you have deprived yourself of your entry to dummy for no reason whatever. By winning the first with the ace or king you leave yourself a choice later.

With (b) there is a bewildering array of possibilities. First you must decide where you need the lead at the first trick. If in dummy, you must put the jack on your ten, or if you wish the king on your queen. It would be a bad mistake to play dummy's king on your ten. If you wish to win the first trick in your own hand, you must make up your mind where you will most need entries later in the play. If you may need entries to your hand, win dummy's nine with your ten; but if you may want entries to dummy, you win dummy's nine with your ace. Usually the two cards you play should be touching in rank. To give yourself the maximum flexibility (i.e. choice later in the play) you try to keep a position in which the sequence of high cards remaining alternates between the two hands. Do not leave one hand with touching high cards.

93

♠

♣

With (c) your choices are simpler. From the last chapter you know that you must "duck" twice, losing two cheap tricks hoping that the opposing cards are split 3-2. You then make a trick with a small card. The point to watch is that you can win the fourth trick in either hand. If you want to end in your hand we save dummy's two until the end. If you want to end in dummy you throw the two earlier.

The Hold Up

94

You should rarely be in a hurry to win a certain trick, or even two certain tricks, in the enemy suit.

West	_East_
♠ A K 6 3	♠ 7 4 2
♡ A 8 6	♡ 5 2
◇ K 9 2	◇ A 6 5
♣ Q 4 3	♣ A J 10 9 7

Again West plays in three notrump (bidding 1 NT-3 NT) and North leads the king of hearts.

It is easy to see that you can gather nine tricks: four or five in clubs, and five top tricks in the other suits. The danger is that the opponents will make the king of clubs and four or five heart tricks.

North presumably has a long suit of hearts (at least four cards). If so, you can make your nine tricks with complete certainty. Let North hold the first trick with his heart king, and if he plays another heart, play low again. Save the ace of hearts till the third round of the suit. The complete hand is diagrammed as follows:

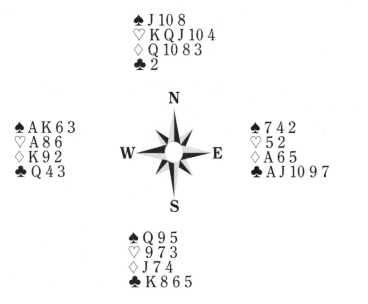

♠ J 10 8
♡ K Q J 10 4
◇ Q 10 8 3
♣ 2

♠ A K 6 3
♡ A 8 6
◇ K 9 2
♣ Q 4 3

♠ 7 4 2
♡ 5 2
◇ A 6 5
♣ A J 10 9 7

♠ Q 9 5
♡ 9 7 3
◇ J 7 4
♣ K 8 6 5

If you study the diagram, you will see that if West wins the first or second heart trick he will be defeated. If he saves his ace till the third round he is safe. By doing this he cuts the enemy communications: when South wins his king of clubs he has no more hearts to lead to his partner, and North's two established winners are useless to him.

Notice that if the defenders play a diamond early, West must win in his own hand, preserving dummy's ace as a valuable entry.

This type of hold-up play is almost always right in a notrump contract. Generally speaking, you should hold up automatically unless you fear the defense will play another suit in which you are weak. The hold-up will not always gain, but it will very seldom show a loss.

♣

When to Draw Trumps

Suppose you are playing in a trump contract, and you have a sound trump fit: five cards in your hand, and three cards in dummy. The first question you must ask yourself is: "Do I draw trumps?"

Nearly always you can answer that question by looking at dummy's shortest suit, and then compare it with the same suit in your own hand.

The following rule has many exceptions, but it will serve as a working basis:

> *If you have more cards than dummy in dummy's short suit, do* NOT *draw trumps.*
>
> *But if your hand is just as short or shorter than dummy's short suit, draw trumps.*

Here is a very simple example:

West	*East*
♠ A K Q 7 5	♠ J 6 3
♡ 8 4	♡ J 6
◇ A 5 2	◇ K 7 4
♣ K 8 4	♣ Q J 10 5 2

West is playing in four spades (bidding: 1♠ -2♠ -3♠ -4♠) and the defenders win two heart tricks and lead a diamond.

Should you draw trumps? Dummy's shortage is in hearts, and you are equally short, so you draw trumps. There is nothing in your hand that you can ruff (trump) in dummy, so dummy's trumps are useless, and you are content to see them disappear.

Win the diamond in your own hand, saving dummy's king as a valuable entry to the weak hand. Then play trumps until the defenders' trumps are exhausted. Their five cards in trumps are likely to split 3-2, but they may be 4 -1 so be careful to play the jack of spades first – the high card from the short hand. Then it is simple to play clubs, playing the king first, so that West's losing diamond can be discarded on a winning club in dummy.

♦

West	_East_
♠ A Q J 9 4	♠ K 10 5
♡ 6 2	♡ A K 8 7 5
◇ 10 9 4	◇ Q 7
♣ A K 7	♣ J 4 3

Again West is playing four spades and North leads the two of clubs.

You have nine sure tricks: five in spades, two in hearts and two in clubs. Where can you find a tenth? There is an immediate chance in clubs. If North has the queen of clubs, dummy's jack can win the first trick; so you play the jack but unfortunately South kills it with his club queen.

Should you draw trumps? Dummy's shortage is in diamonds, and declarer has more diamonds than dummy, so this is a hand on which you do not draw trumps. You have a chance of ruffing a diamond in dummy, and if you can ruff in the shorter trump hand (usually dummy) you gain a trick. So lead a diamond. Whatever the opponents do, then lead another diamond. Later lead your last diamond, and trump it in dummy with a high spade. Your tenth trick has arrived.

If the defenders had been very clever they might have defeated the contract by leading a spade originally. If they keep leading trumps, dummy's trumps disappear before you can ruff a diamond. This is perfectly logical. If it pays you not to lead trumps, it will probably pay the defenders to lead trumps. Notice also that it does not help West to trump a heart. His long trumps are going to be tricks anyway, and you have already counted on five trump tricks. Normally it only helps to trump in the short trump hand.

Sometimes you must postpone drawing trumps because you need to do something else in a hurry:

West	_East_
♠ K Q J 7 4	♠ 10 8 3
♡ K 6	♡ Q J 2
◇ K 5 4	◇ A 8 7 3
♣ Q 9 3	♣ K J 6

97

♣

Again West is in four spades and North leads the queen of diamonds.

Prospects look rosy. You should be able to make four trump tricks, and two tricks in each side-suit. The opponents will make just their three aces.

Take a look at the diamond suit. When the ace and king have gone, you will lose a trick there. But you can discard this loser on a heart from dummy; when dummy's second heart trick makes you will be out of hearts, and can discard the losing diamond. But we must get the discard quickly, before the defenders can make a diamond trick.

So win the diamond lead with the king, and play the king of hearts. If this holds, play another heart. Now if the defenders play another diamond you can win in dummy, cash the heart queen, and discard your last diamond. Now you can start to play trumps, and any further diamond lead can be trumped. Unless you are very unlucky all you will lose will be the three aces.

Normally on such a hand you would draw trumps at once, because dummy has no useful shortage, or indeed any shortage. But if you look ahead you can see that to play trumps would lead to certain defeat. The defenders win the ace of spades and play a second diamond. Now you are sure to lose a diamond and three aces, and dummy's extra heart trick will be established too late to be of any value.

Wealth In Trumps

If you are lucky enough to be loaded with trumps you can draw the few enemy trumps immediately more often.* If you have nine or more trumps in the combined hands, with at least four in each hand, there will seldom be any hurry to get one ruff in the short trump hand. You can draw trumps and get the ruff later.

Sometimes having trumps to spare turns out to have a special advantage:

West	*East*
♠ A K 7 6 4	♠ Q 10 9 5 3
♡ A 4	♡ 8 6
◇ Q 7 4	◇ J 6 2
♣ A Q 7	♣ K 8 5

98

---

* — Conversely, if your trump holding is feeble you should hardly ever try to draw trumps. Suppose your trump suit is K x x x opposite J x x; leave the trumps along, play on the other suits, and hope to come to a trump trick or two "in the wash."

Again you are in four spades, and North leads the king of hearts. This hand is annoying because the two hands have identical patterns. The heart shortage is useless and nothing can be ruffed anywhere. This is known as duplication, and is enough to make any declarer bad-tempered.

You must lose a heart and two diamonds, and may well lose three diamonds. We saw in the last chapter that this diamond combination is one we would like the opponents to lead. So you win the ace of hearts, draw trumps, cash the three club tricks, and play a heart.

Assuming you have had to play three rounds of trumps, the position will now be this:

♠ 7 6   ♠ 10 9
♡ —   ♡ —
◇ Q 7 4   ◇ J 6 2
♣ —   ♣ —

One of the defenders will have the lead – and will wish that he had not. Whatever he does will help you. If he leads a diamond you are certain to make a diamond trick. If he plays a heart or a club, you get a ruff-and-discard: you can ruff in either hand, and discard a diamond from the other hand. Then you lose only two diamond tricks.

This type of play is knows as"elimination," and occurs in a variety of situations. The general idea is to give the opponents the lead when anything they do will help you. In the preceding example it was essential to play the clubs before the heart, for otherwise the defender could safely lead a club. Normally in such situations you should clear any side-suit in which you have obvious tricks to cash.

West	*East*
♠ A K J 6	♠ Q 10 4 2
♡ —	♡ Q 10 8 6 3
◇ K 9 8 7 4	◇ —
♣ A 10 8 6	♣ K 7 4 3

99

♣   The contract is again four spades, and North leads the ace of hearts. The bidding went 1◇-1♡-1♠-2♠-3♣-4♠ . (West's 3 assets disappear when his partner bids hearts, but come back to life when the spade fit is found. Three clubs invites game, and East accepts.)

Outside the trump suit you have only two sure tricks; but the ruffing possibilities are splendid. Trump the opening lead, cash the ace and king of clubs, and then trump red cards backwards and forwards indefinitely. This is a complete cross-ruff: all the eight trumps you have are made separately.

An important general rule on such hands is to make the sure outside tricks before starting to cross-ruff. If on the above hand you fail to make your club winners first, they might never make. A defender might be able to discard a club or two while you are cross-ruffing, and trump one of your winners. Notice also that an opening trump lead would have defeated the contract, as two of your valuable trumps would fall on the same trick.

100

Establishing A Suit By Ruffing

In a trump contract you can often establish tricks in a suit by ruffing tricks which would have been lost at notrump.

	(a)		(b)		(c)
Dummy has:	A K x x x		A Q x x x		A Q J 10
Declarer has:	x x		x		x

These are all side-suits in a trump contract. If we had (a) in a notrump contract we would duck a trick and hope the suit split 3-3. But with trumps available you can play ace and king and then trump a low card. Now if the suit has split 3-3 you have two winners in dummy, and you have not lost a trick. If the suit splits 4-2 you can, entries permitting, ruff dummy's fourth card to make the fifth a winner.

♦

The play on (b) depends on the entry position, and on how many tricks you need. If you need only two tricks and have plenty of entries, simply keep trumping until the king appears. But if you need three tricks from the suit, or need two tricks and are short of entries, it is best to finesse the queen.

With (c) you can take a "ruffing finesse." Play to the ace and lead the queen, hoping the king is on the right. Unless the king appears on the right you discard losers, and with luck can make three tricks in the suit without losing the lead.

There are many advanced techniques in dummy-play which we cannot hope to cover in a book of this length; but if you can apply sensibly the ideas in the last two chapters you will have a good foundation for successful play as declarer.

Quiz

1. The opening lead is the 2, and you have the following:

Dummy
K Q 10
2 led
You
A J 9

How should you play if:

(a)   You want to win the first trick in your own hand?
(b)   You want to win the first trick in dummy?

2.   In the following cases you are West playing in four spades. Say whether you should draw trumps, and briefly plan the play.

102

(a)
West		**East**
♠ Q J 10 7 5	◇ K led	♠ K 9 3
♡ A K 6		♡ Q 2
◇ A 9 7		◇ 8 5 4
♣ 8 3		♣ A J 10 6 2

(b)
West		**East**
♠ Q J 10 7 5	◇ K led	♠ K 8 3
♡ A K 6		♡ Q 2
◇ A 9 7		◇ 8 5 4
♣ 8 3		♣ A K 10 6 2

(c)
West		**East**
♠ K J 9 7 4	◇ K led	♠ Q 10 8 6 3
♡ —		♡ A 7 5 4
◇ A 10 5		◇ 9 7 3 2
♣ 10 9 8 6 4		♣ —

Quiz Answers

♥

1. (a)   Play the king or queen from dummy and cover with your ace.

    (b)   Play the king or queen from dummy, and play the nine from your hand. In each case you leave an "interlocked" position, which gives you the greatest flexibility.

2. (a)   Do not draw trumps. You must plan to ruff a diamond in dummy. Best is to duck the first trick, win the second diamond, and play three rounds of hearts discarding dummy's last diamond. Now you can play to your ace of diamonds and ruff your last diamond. This gives you ten tricks.

    (b)   You could play as in (a) but this is slightly risky. As you only need ten tricks it is safest to draw trumps at once, and make no effort to make eleven tricks.

103

    (c)   Do not draw trumps. Play a cross-ruff, backwards and forwards in clubs and hearts.

♠

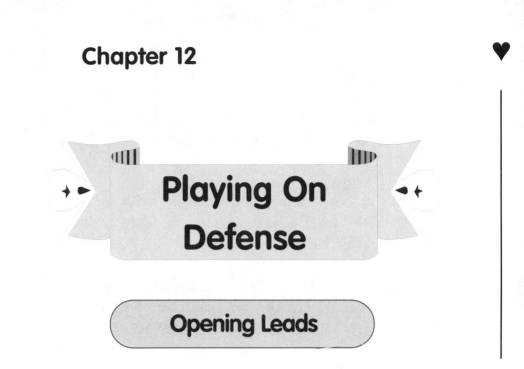

Chapter 12

Playing On Defense

Opening Leads

The basic rules for leading are:

(i) The top card of a sequence headed by an honor (K Q J). Exception: From A K, lead the king unless it is a doubleton. (However, some players lead the ace from A K, so discuss it with your partner.)

(ii) The top card of a worthless suit (7 4 2) or of any doubleton (Q 2). (However, some players lead small with three small cards, so discuss it with your partner.)

(iii) The fourth best (i.e. fourth from the top) of any four-card or longer suit, or the third best of a three-card suit. (K 7 4 2; or K 7 4 3 2; or K 3 2.) (These rules apply not only on the opening lead, but at any later point in the play.)

Defending notrump you should normally lead your longest suit, especially if it is a five-card suit or longer. With three honor cards, two of which are in sequence, lead the higher of the touching cards: A J 10 x x; A Q J x x; or K J 10 x. With less than three honor cards normally lead the fourth best card. If your longest suit has only four cards it may be unwise to lead it.

♣

The following leads are distinctly undesirable:

J x x x   **A Q x x**   **Q x x x**   **A J x x**

The next group are better, but still not very attractive:

A x x x   **K x x x**   **K J x x**   **Q 10 x x**

Rather than lead a scrappy suit of this kind, it may well be better to lead the top card of a worthless suit. This is a passive move, made partly in the hope that it may be partner's suit, but mainly because it is unlikely to give the declarer a trick.

If your partner has bid a suit you should nearly always lead it. Lead the normal card, as indicated above.* Only lead your own suit if it is a good suit, and you have an entry to run the suit when established. A K x x x or A Q x x x are definitely good leads. If your partner returns the suit later you are likely to make four tricks.

106

If in doubt, it often pays to lead the unbid major suit. If the opponents have bid one major and not the other, your partner will often hold the one they have not bid.

At notrump the defenders usually want to attack, and try to establish a long suit. But defending a trump contract the situation is very different. The main consideration now is safety.

Against a suit contract never underlead an ace: if one opponent has a singleton you will probably never make your ace.

Any honor holding with gaps is an undesirable lead now, whatever the length of the suit. Suits headed by A Q, or A J 10, or K J 10, which were satisfactory against notrump, should be avoided.

The only good leads from an honor holding are those containing two touching honors, preferably with another in close support:

A K J or K Q J or K Q 10 or Q J 10 or Q J 9 or J 10 9 are good leads.

These are reasonable: **A K x or K Q x or Q J x or J 10 x**

◆

As at notrump, the top card of a worthless suit is a reasonable passive lead, particularly if it is a suit bid by dummy. If your partner has bid a suit, you still normally lead his suit, but make sure you lead the ace if you have it.

A trump lead is usually safe, and often of positive value, especially if you judge that declarer will be trying for ruffs in dummy. There were two hands in the last chapter in which a trump lead would have killed the contract. A good defender would probably have led a trump in each case.

Signalling

Frequently a defender will feel a strong urge to lean across the table and give his partner a firm instruction about the best way to conduct the defense. Fortunately for the declarer the laws of the game prohibit such a brazen communication, but with more legality and more subtlety the message can usually be transmitted just the same. Often the defender is in a position in which his choice of card to play matters very little. In such cases he can generally choose a card which will give guidance to his partner.

(i) **Sequences.** With a holding such as K Q J or Q J 10 you already know that you must lead the highest card, either as the first lead or later in the play. But if one of the other players leads the suit, you should play the lowest card of your sequence.

Suppose your opening lead is the two from K 7 4 2. Dummy has three small cards, and your partner plays the jack which declarer wins with the ace. You now know with certainty that your partner has the queen, for otherwise declarer would have played it; you also know with certainty that declarer has the ten, for otherwise your partner would have played it. If you follow suit with a high card you clearly deny the next lower card.

If both players play the correct card on defense, many valuable deductions of this kind can be drawn.

♣

(ii) **Encouraging.** To ask your partner to play a suit, or to continue playing a suit, you play an *unnecessarily high card* in that suit.

Suppose against notrump your partner leads a king, and you hold A 9 8 2. You want him to continue, but it would be overly extravagant to play your ace. You play the nine — *the highest card you can spare.* Usually the encouraging signal is made with a high card, but if you have, for example, A 3 2 the best you can do is to play the three. Partner should be able to work it out when the two does not appear. You would also play an encouraging card if you had the jack: play the nine from J 9 8 2, or the three from J 3 2. With an honor sequence you can be very positive. If you throw the jack, you show the ten and deny holding the queen.

If partner leads a king against a suit contract, you can play high-low with a doubleton if you think he has the ace. He will continue, and you will be able to ruff the third round of the suit.

Similarly you can make an encouraging signal when discarding on a suit in which you have no more cards. Usually the best you can do is to throw a medium-high card, such as a seven or an eight, to ask partner to lead a particular suit. But if you have an honor sequence, you throw the top card of the sequence: if you throw a king your partner knows you have the queen and jack and have not got the ace.

(iii) **Discouraging.** This is the obvious converse of the last section. If you play your lowest possible card, you warn partner against playing a suit. Sometimes this can be especially useful. Suppose you are discarding on a club suit, and want to ask your partner to play diamonds – but you may not wish to part with a diamond. All your diamonds may be useful to you. By throwing your lowest spade and then your lowest heart, you give your partner an indirect suggestion to play diamonds.

Encouraging and discouraging is the basis of bridge signalling. But sometimes, when it is clear that you cannot want to encourage or discourage, your small cards can be made to carry other special messages.

108

♦

iv) **Showing length.** If dummy has a strong suit which is being played, it will often help your partner to know how many cards you hold in the suit. With three cards (or just possibly with five) you play your lowest card. With two cards or four cards you play a high card:

♠ K Q J 10 6
(*North*)
Dummy

♣ A 8 7
(*East*)

You are East, defending a notrump contract, and dummy's only asset is its good spades. To get the best out of the defense you must arrange to put your ace on the declarer's last spade: certainly no sooner, and preferably no later. If West's first card is the two, you can be sure he has three cards. Declarer must have a doubleton, so you "hold-up" your ace once and win the second trick. Now dummy's remaining spades are dead. But if West plays the four, and follows with the three or the two, you know he has a doubleton, and you must save your ace till the third round of the suit.

(v) **Suit preference.** Suppose you are defending four spades, and during the bidding the opponents have bid and supported diamonds. You have to lead from this hand: ♠ 4   ♡ J 8 5 2   ◇ A 10 7 5 2   ♣ A 6 4. You have a happy thought: your partner *must* be short in diamonds. So you lead the ace of diamonds followed by another diamond which he will ruff. He can put you in the lead with your ace of clubs, and you give him another diamond ruff.

Unfortunately the best defense is not so clear to your partner. When he ruffs the second trick he plays a heart. Declarer wins, draws trumps, and makes his contract. How was poor partner to know you had the ace of clubs? The answer is that you tell him by playing the *two* of

♠

♣

diamonds as your second lead. As this is your lowest diamond, it asks him to play the *lower* of the side-suits. If you had the ace of hearts instead of the ace of clubs, your second lead would be the *ten* of diamonds. (If you had no other ace and did not much mind what partner did, you would play a middle diamond.)

This is a suit preference signal, which often allows you to ask partner for one of the two side-suits. But remember that it can only apply if there is no question of encouraging and discouraging.

(vi) **Signal in Trumps**. A signal of rather rare value is the play of an unnecessarily high trump. This tells partner that you have exactly three trumps and wish to ruff another suit.

Second Low and Third High

110

Although there are many exceptions, the old whist rule that second player plays low and third player plays high is a useful basis for the defense in bridge.

The business of high cards is to kill the enemy high cards. If declarer leads a small card and the second player wins the trick with an ace or king the power of the high card is wasted. It will collect a trick with only small cards in it, when it should probably be killing a queen or a jack. If you have a powerful holding like K Q J x x, by all means play the jack. But in all normal situations, unless you have a very strong reason for not doing so, play low second in hand, and play low *quickly*. Many tricks are given away be defenders who are in too much of a hurry to win with an ace; even *thinking* about winning with the ace may be a bad mistake.

Third hand high, when dummy is on your right and your partner has led, is largely common sense. If dummy has small cards only, you can apply the rule automatically, remembering to play the lowest card of a sequence (K Q, or Q J 10). If partner leads the jack, and you have the ace only or the king only, you must play your high card. You know declarer has the queen, but if that is his only high card he must be prevented from making it.

♦

The situation is very different if dummy has one or two high cards. Now you must save your high cards to kill the high cards in dummy. If partner leads the jack and dummy has the queen, you must play low with the ace or king unless the queen is played. The business of your ace or king is to kill dummy's queen. The following are more advanced applications of the same principle:

K x x	Q x x	J x x
Dummy	**Dummy**	**Dummy**
2 led A J x	2 led K 10 x	2 led Q 9 x
(a)	**(b)**	**(c)**

In each case your partner leads the two and dummy plays low. With (a) you play the jack. With (b) you play the ten. With (c) you play the nine. You must save your high card to kill the high card in dummy later. There are many such positions, but the principle is always the same.

111

Covering Honors

The business of your high cards, and this cannot be repeated too often, is to kill the high cards in the hand on your right. So if your right-hand opponent leads a high card and you can kill it you usually do so. The object of covering is to try to promote a trick in your hand or your partner's hand. If you bear this in mind it is not difficult to see that there are some cases in which covering cannot help.

Consider the following examples:

A x x		A x x	
Dummy		**Dummy**	
K J 10	(a)	K 9 x	(b)
You		**You**	
Q led		Q led	

♣

With (a) it is easy to see that you must kill the queen with your king. Your jack and ten are then established as winners. They have been *promoted*, like a junior officer on the battlefield, by the wholesale slaughter of the top three honors.

With (b) you must cover also. This time you do not know who has the jack and ten, but you must hope your partner has at least one of them. If he has both, he will have two promoted winners. If he has neither, your side will not make a trick whatever you do.

	A J 10 9 x			A J 9 x x	
	Dummy			Dummy	
K x x		(c)	K x x		(d)
You			You		
	Q led			Q led	

(c) is an obvious example in which you should not cover. As you can see the jack, ten and nine in dummy, killing the queen with your king cannot possibly help your side. Your only hope of stopping the declarer from making five tricks is that his queen is a singleton.

But with (d) you must cover and hope your partner has the ten. If he has, it will stop the run of the suit and probably take a trick; work out what happens if the declarer has one small card only. If the declarer has the ten, there is nothing you can do.

	A x			A x x x	
	Dummy			Dummy	
K x x		(e)	Q x x		(f)
	Q led			J led	

With (e) you should play low. When declarer leads the queen he is very likely indeed to have the jack. As dummy has only a doubleton, your king will survive to be a master on the third round of the suit.

In (f) also you should play low, and play low *quickly*, because covering is unlikely to help your partner and may well help the declarer.

♦

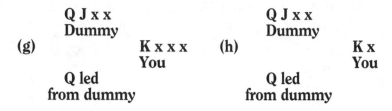

A general rule is that you do not cover an honor that is part of a sequence. In (g) the queen and jack are in sequence, so you should play low: the killing power of your king can be reserved for the jack.

But in (h) you must cover the queen because you cannot afford to wait. If declarer has the ace your king will die, but it will die in any case. If you play low, a small card may follow and your king will do no work at all; but if you kill the queen at once it may help your partner.

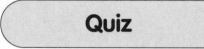

113

1. What card would you lead from each of the following suits?
(a) J 10 9 4.   **(b) Q 10 9 8.**   **(c) 8 3.**   **(d) Q 10 7 3 2.**

2. You hold a suit consisting of Q J 10 9 8. What card do you play in the suit if:
   (a) it is your opening lead?
   (b) your partner has led and you have to follow suit?
   (c) if you have to make a discard, and you want your partner to lead the suit?
   (d) If you have the make a discard and you want to make your partner lead another suit?

♣

3. Your partner leads against three notrump and dummy plays a small card. What card do you play in each of the following:

Q x x	**x** x x	**A J** x
Dummy	**Dummy**	**Dummy**
2 led **A 10** x	J led **K** x x	2 led **K 10** x
You	**You**	**You**
(a)	**(b)**	**(c)**

4. An honor card is led and you can cover it with a higher honor. Say whether or not you should cover in each of the following cases:

A K x	**A J** x x	**J 10** x
Dummy	**Dummy**	**Dummy**
Q x x x **(a)**	**K** x x **(b)** **(c)**	**Q** x x
You	**You**	**J led from**
J led	**Q led**	**Dummy**

114

Quiz Answers

1. (a) Jack. (b) Ten. (c) Eight. (d) Three.

2. (a) Queen. (b) Eight. (c) Queen. (d) Eight. (The eight may look like an encouraging card, but it is the best you can do. Partner should work it out: he can see a lot of the smaller cards in his hand and dummy.)

3. (a) Ten. (b) King. (c) Ten.

4. (a) No. Declarer may well have J 10 9 x and if you wait your queen will control the fourth round of the suit.
    (b) Yes. You must hope your partner has the ten.
    (c) No. Dummy's jack and ten form a sequence, so save your queen to kill the ten.

♦

Chapter 13

♥

What Next?

Now that you understand the basics of bridge, consider the following possibilities.

1. Collect three others who would like to play, sit down and do it. If somebody claims ignorance, make him or her read this book. If possible, plan a regular game, perhaps once a week.

2. Do some more reading. Two books that will take the reader a step further in bridge understanding are: *Basic Bridge in Three Weeks* by Alan Truscott (Putnam); *Bid Better, Play Better* by Dorothy Truscott (Devyn Press).

3. Join the American Contract Bridge League (A.C.B.L.) Address 2990 Airways Blvd., Memphis, TN 38116 Telephone: (901) 332-5586. Web Site: www.acbl.org (Outside North America, go to the Web Site: www.bridge.gr).

4. Visit a local club. If the yellow pages do not give an answer, ask the A.C.B.L. for a Club Directory.

5. Your local club probably has activities for novices. Ask about them.

6. Take a lesson. This may be group instruction, or a playing lesson in which an expert player is your partner for an afternoon or evening.

♠

7. Visit a tournament. The A.C.B.L. or your local club can tell you where and when. There will be novice games, and perhaps lectures.

8. Watch an expert, but do it quietly. The tournament director will point out an expert who is worth "kibitzing".

9. Buy a program that will allow you to play bridge with and against the computer. The three best American programs are at the following Web Sites:

   www.gibware.com
   www.bridgebaron.com
   rrnet.com/meadowlark

10. Buy a program that will improve your skill. Bridgemaster is one of many available from Baron Barclay, Telephone: 1-800-274-2221.

And if you have internet access you can:

11. Join an online club that will allow you to play bridge at any time with partners and opponents around the world. The two leading clubs are:
    OKbridge.com
    e-bridgemaster.com

Finale

♣ ◆ ♥ ♠

It is not possible in a book of this length
to deal with the higher strategy of the game. We have
dealt with the rules, the structure of bidding, and the
basic tactics of play and defense. If you, the reader, have
absorbed this and can apply it fairly well you will already
be better equipped than very many bridge-players.
What is more, you will probably win.

I hope you do!

Notes:

_____

_____

_____

_____

_____

_____

_____

_____

_____

_____

_____

_____

_____

_____

_____